Tragedy is when I cut my finger.
Comedy is when you fall into an open sewer and die.

—MEL BROOKS

SALES INSANITY

20 True Stories of Epic Sales Blunders
(and how to avoid them yourself)

Jason Jordan

Published by
Ivy House Publishing

Sales Insanity / Jason Jordan. – 2nd edition
ISBN 978-0-9980598-2-2 (paperback)
ISBN 978-0-9980598-1-5 (e-book)

Dedicated to my wife – the best editor ever, because she's not afraid to tell me I wrote something stupid.

CONTENTS

PART IV: LET'S KEEP THE PARTY GOING

REFERENCE GUIDE: JUST THE GOOD IDEAS

FOREWORD

From an early age, we are advised that we should learn from our mistakes. In fact, we're taught that we will learn our most valuable lessons 'the hard way'—by making our own missteps and directly suffering the consequences. Not only do I agree with this assertion, I know it to be true.

Many of the fundamental principles that currently guide my day-to-day decisions were discovered early in my career as I naively made one error in judgment after another. This is what young people do. So I did. And when the missteps resulted in consequences that were dire enough, the lessons were stamped indelibly into my memory. For instance:

THE STORY OF MONSIEURS FREY AND MORRIS

One of my earliest and most poignant examples of such an experience took place when I was in my 20s. I was a loan officer for a mortgage company—my first job out of college. I was working on a particularly tricky set of home loans for two borrowers whose names were Frey and Morris. (To underscore the impact of this lesson, I still recall their names 25 years later, though I barely remember my own phone number.)

Mr. Frey and Mr. Morris were joint owners of a company, against which they had co-borrowed a single business loan. They wanted to mortgage their individual homes to pay off the business loan, so their company would be free of debt. The challenge in this particular situation was that both of their new personal loans had to close simultaneously, so the existing business loan could be paid off at once. Otherwise, one of the borrowers would unavoidably be exposed to greater financial risk than the other.

Since the two loans had to close simultaneously, it made logical sense to secure the loans from a single lender. Therefore, I submitted both loans to a single bank that I knew rather well, assuming that both loans would secure quick approvals. Unexpectedly, one of the loans was approved while the other one was declined. At the time, I was quite upset with the underwriter. After substantial haggling with her, I indignantly requested that she send *both* of the loans back to me. If she didn't want them both, then she could have neither. I would teach her a lesson.

I then submitted both loans to a second lender that quickly approved the loan that had been denied by the first lender, but the new underwriter *declined* the mortgage that had been previously approved by the first. More haggling ensued to no avail. Now I was both indignant and frustrated, so I again requested that both loans be returned to me. This was yet another uncooperative person to whom I would need to teach a lesson on my way to funding these mortgages.

To make a long story less long, I couldn't find a lender that would accept both loans. And while I was working myself into a lather and doling out lessons to uncooperative underwriters, Frey and Morris eventually lost patience with me. In the end, they took their loans elsewhere, and I lost $3,200 in commissions at a time when $3,200 was a LOT of money to me. It was a painful experience that I spent a long time processing.

If I had just stayed calm and left one loan with the first lender and taken the other loan to the second lender, all would have been fine. The loans would have been delivered on time, and everyone would have been happy. But then, I wouldn't have learned a lesson that has served me well on many occasions: The goal of doing business is not to prevail on a personal level or to dole out lessons to others—the point of doing business is to do business. And from that experience forward, I've been a much better businessman. Monsieurs Frey and Morris have no idea how grateful I am to them for their rightful impatience decades ago. They were the ones who ended up teaching *me* a lesson, and I truly learned it the hard way.

THE PROBLEM WITH LEARNING THE HARD WAY

While there's no doubt in my mind that we learn our most valuable lessons by making our own mistakes and suffering the consequences, there's an inherent problem with this developmental strategy: It's not very scalable. In fact, I can count on my fingers the number of formative experiences I've had that truly shaped the way I think and behave. Yet there are probably dozens of insane things I do every week that I wouldn't do if I only knew better. I just haven't had the privilege of experiencing a painful consequence from them.

Sales Insanity provides a unique opportunity: The freedom to learn from other people's tragic consequences while remaining at a safe distance ourselves. Why lose $3,200 of our own money to learn a new lesson when we can watch some-one else do it for us? We shouldn't have to suffer ourselves to learn a valuable insight. Let someone else take the pain, and let us just take the insight.

I hope you enjoy *Sales Insanity* as much as I enjoyed writing it. It's a great opportunity to learn some valuable lessons without having to endure the associated pain. I expect that you'll recognize a little of yourself in many of these stories, just as I did. Heaven knows, I've flirted with insanity at many points in my career. In fact, I've even crossed that line once or twice. Just ask Monsieurs Frey and Morris.

Jason Jordan

PART I
SALES FORCES
AND
BAD BEHAVIORS

CHAPTER ONE

SALES, CONSULTING, AND BEST PRACTICES

SALES IS THE BEST

I've had a pretty interesting career. If nothing else, it has been fun. I think what's made it so much fun is that I've spent almost all of it working in or around sales forces. My first job after college was a hard-core sales gig. I was given a desk, a phone book, and three months of salary, after which it was a 100% commission, kill-what-you-eat affair. I occasionally went hungry, but mostly I ate well. And I surely had fun.

After a few years of sales excitement, I returned to school for a graduate degree in business and then dutifully became a management consultant. While not in a direct sales role, I ended up doing a lot of interesting work for sales forces around the world. From sales process definition, to Customer Relationship Management (CRM) implementation, to territory alignment, to incentive plan design, I worked with senior sales leadership to ask the right questions, find the best answers, and then carefully manage change.

From that point in my career, I bounced back and forth between the two vocations—first sales, then consulting, then back to sales, then back to consulting. But since college, I've never had a job that wasn't in or around the sales force. As far as I'm concerned, sales is the best.

EXCEPT FOR THE INSANITY

However, sales is also the part of any company where the most ridiculous stuff takes place. Literally, things happen in the sales force that are so unexpectedly wrong, it's often hard to comprehend what you're seeing. You step back and look at what's taking place, and you can't help but think to yourself, "Is that person insane?" Of course they're not—yet they just did something that makes you wonder. So why is this silliness so prevalent in the sales force?

First, there is no formal education for people entering the sales profession. Only a handful of colleges and universities offer any standard coursework in sales, so folks like me who go into sales are forced to figure it out on their own. This form of knowledge acquisition is also known as "trial and error," and it's a hard way to learn. Sure salespeople receive a fair amount of training, but it is typically more focused on tactical skills than strategic decision making. As careers progress randomly down a trial-and-error development path, bad decisions get made as a matter of course.

Second, sales is an uncontrolled environment. Unlike manufacturing or operations where the inputs and processes are tightly controlled, sales forces have to deal with the most unpredictable of inputs—customers. No matter how competent and sane the salespeople might be, they will constantly encounter unexpected and unpredictable situations. And then they react the best way they can, which often presents itself as insanity. But then, if it weren't for the customers and their completely random behaviors, how much fun would sales really be?

ON BEING A CONSULTANT

Of the career I've split between sales and consulting, most of you will associate more closely with my years spent carrying a quota. However, it's worth explaining the perspective I gained as a management consultant, because many of the stories that follow are told from that viewpoint: the viewpoint of someone who is hired on a temporary basis to solve problems that are painful enough for executives to seek outside help.

Whether you like consultants, hate them, or are wholly indifferent, there's a lot of value in being a knowledgeable outsider. First, a consultant is able to look at existing problems with fresh a set of eyes. It's like the kind of vision you have when a friend describes his family problems to you. You can look at the issues a little more dispassionately and assess them a little more objectively than he's capable of doing himself. So a consultant can frequently recognize insane behavior a little more quickly and describe it a little more frankly than an active participant in the fray.

Another advantage of bringing in a temporary troubleshooter is that consultants work with lots of different companies. This experience allows them to see patterns of behavior across many organizations. While every company is of course a little unique, the truth is that most business problems are fairly similar. A seasoned consultant can not only pick the usual suspects out of a lineup, he can almost predict the insanity before it happens ... because it inevitably does. If you want to observe a lot of deviant business behavior, you should seriously consider a career in consulting.

A RANT AGAINST "BEST PRACTICES"

Early in my consulting career, I worked for a very large accounting firm that had built a hugely profitable consulting practice. One of the ongoing initiatives in the consulting group was to build a comprehensive database of business "Best Practices." This database included strategies and tactics for any business activity you could imagine—how to process an invoice, how to resolve a customer complaint, how to manage payroll, and most other things that businesses must do.

The value of this database, I determined, was twofold. First, this database made us better consultants, because it institutionalized the learned knowledge of thousands of experts. In theory, a new consultant could come onboard and begin to dispense sage advice to clients with the same level of insight as a seasoned consultant. All that was needed was smart, confident employees with the ability to pose the right questions to the database.

The second source of value derived from this database, though, was much greater than just enabling an army of inexperienced consultants to sound smart. It also enabled us to be better sellers. "Well, Mr. Prospect, when you hire our firm, you will have access to our proprietary database of global Best Practices collected from leading companies around the world that found unexpected and innovative ways to solve the precise problem that is currently crippling your business." The database ostensibly held valuable insight that they needed but didn't have.

Yet even in my earliest days as a consultant, I began to question the value of these touchstone Best Practices. As I worked with more and more clients and tried to apply the practices to specific situations, I saw flaws in the logic that there's a single best answer to every similar-looking question. I discovered that despite the allure of having a definitive body of guiding business principles, these universal practices were just too generic to account for every situation. What's right in one instance is not necessarily right in another.

It didn't take many failed attempts to apply these global principles to specific situations before I reached the conclusion that there are, in fact, no global Best Practices with a capital B and capital P. There are simply common business practices that may or may not be applicable, depending on the particular situation. In my eyes, the Best Practice myth was therefore dispelled. And once you've seen through a charade, you can never believe in it again.

EXECUTIVE COMFORT FOOD

Unfortunately, at about the same time that I purged the defeated Best Practices from my consulting toolkit, the rest of the world caught Best Practice fever. Consulting firms and research clearinghouses began to fan the flames of the Best Practice fire with great fervor. The Best Practice became its own industry with hundreds of millions of dollars spent each year by executives that *needed* access to the capital B and P. And so it remains today.

The Best Practice is now the single piece of information that everyone needs to know before they can make any meaningful business decision. To make a key decision without knowing *the* Best Practice is foolhardy, at best. At worst, you're a negligent executive who has imperiled your company by ignoring the demonstrated wisdom of others. It seems that doing your own thinking when someone else has already done it for you can jeopardize your entire career.

I exaggerate this point only modestly. It would be impossible for me to describe how often I got questions about the "Current Best Practices" during the course of any consulting day. (Best Practices have been around long enough that savvy executives now must know the *Current* Best Practices ... with a capital C.) Just off the top of my head, here a few requests I received from clients over and over again:

- "Could you tell us the Current Best Practices in sales compensation?"
- "What are the Current Best Practices for implementing CRM?"
- "What sales process is currently considered a Best Practice?"

Believe me, I could fill pages with such questions—none of which have a one-size-fits-all legitimate answer.

Alas, despite all the logic I could present to discredit the capital B, P, and now C, I am resigned to the fact they are a part of our business lexicon, and I will probably never live to see the demand for those letters subside. I have instead tried to understand what it is that drives this ubiquitous obsession, and I've derived a couple of plausible reasons.

First, it's corporate voyeurism, pure and simple. As the consequence of some unquenchable curiosity, executives desperately want to see what other companies are doing—especially the doings of their competitors. Everybody wants a glimpse behind the curtain, just to see what's there.

I liken it to my wife's and my compulsion to attend open houses in our own neighborhood. For years we've watched those houses and wondered what's inside; therefore, we *must* take advantage of the opportunity to peek inside and see what they've done to justify their eye-popping asking price. Did they remodel their kitchen with upgraded appliances? Are their floors tile or stone? Regardless of what we find, we probably won't remodel our own house to match. But it sure is fun to look.

Second, I think Best Practices reflect the desire for an easy fix. Everyone wants quick and simple answers to our most complex questions. What could be more appealing than the idea that someone else has already gone through the messy and time-consuming process of examining all the alternatives, implementing a solution, making the obvious mistakes, refining the plan, and finally declaring success? Even better, Best Practices offer the illusion of reducing the risk of failure, because someone else has already done it successfully. Honestly, how could it get any better?

So basically, the gravitational pull of the Best Practice is too great to escape. We're led to believe that we can succeed more easily by retracing someone else's footsteps to greatness. It's a one-size-fits-all, silver-bullet bonanza. No matter that the silver bullets were first fired from someone else's gun at someone else's target. Just give it a shot and see what happens. It's a Best Practice.

SAYS A FRIEND ...

Since I concede that Best Practices are here to stay, I will close my rant with an attempt to at least recast it in a more palatable light. I have a colleague who used to work for a prominent research firm that identified and published the Current Best Practices for sales forces. He's an extremely bright person whose opinion I respect, so one morning over breakfast I decided to ask his perspective on the value of the Best Practice.

Treading carefully, I inquired, "So what is it that you think your company actually sells to your customers?" As expected, he had a response that was as elegant as it was accurate. "I've thought about that question quite a bit," he responded. "I believe that what we ultimately offer our clients is 'ideas.' Obviously, we can't tell an executive that any given 'Best Practice' is the absolute right way to run her business. It's just an option that she might not have thought about, and it could be a valuable input to her decision-making process."

Ideas. I like it. We can call them Best Practices with capital letters if we want, just to make them marketable and to give them more gravity. That's fine. But can we all agree that they're not universally applicable incarnations of the single correct way to run every business? They're just *good ideas*. Maybe I *will* install stainless steel appliances because the nicest house in my neighborhood has them ... maybe not. Maybe you *should* implement CRM in five phases because that's how your competitor did it ... maybe not. But it's an idea.

So forget Best Practices for now. Whether or not you believe in them is for you to decide. However, I'd like to introduce something that I think could be much less controversial and much more fun. I offer to the world ... The Worst Practice.

CHAPTER TWO

INTRODUCING THE WORST PRACTICE

THE GENESIS OF THIS BOOK

I was at the home of a long-time friend, where we were working our way through some perfectly grilled steaks and wonderful red wine. I was going on and on about the epic failures that I'd observed at my clients, all the while enjoying the folly of the unwitting salespeople and the slapdash judgment of their management. Perhaps (probably) it was the wine, but the stories were all too entertaining to us both.

The tales all followed a similar storyline: Someone did something that was unknowingly dumb (which is kind of funny), and that led to an unexpected and tragic consequence (making it even funnier). Of course, the tragedy could have been avoided completely, if only the person had recognized something that was completely obvious (which made them appear insane). Failure, after failure, after failure.

After I had recounted a fair number of these vignettes, I jokingly pronounced that, indeed, I would write a book about all the insanity I had observed during my career. After all, what good was such an accumulation of knowledge, if it were not shared with others? How unfair it would be to know and not to tell. The world *must* hear these tales! Indeed, I would write a book. Please pass the wine.

As the haze began to dissipate the following morning (please pass the aspirin), I reconsidered this tome that I had promised to deliver to the world only 12 hours prior. Despite my late-night revelation, was this actually a good idea? A series of questions came to mind.

WORTH WRITING?

What am I really talking about here? Bad salespeople? No. Bad managers? Probably not. Bad companies? Not necessarily. I'm talking about bad *ideas*. Very bad ideas. Ideas that are so misguided there is no plausible circumstance in which they can ever be interpreted as the right things to do. If a good idea can be characterized as a Best Practice, then these are the perfect foil: the bad ideas. The *Worst* Practices.

Except that unlike Best Practices, Worst Practices are not bound by any qualifiers or caveats—they are just wrong. They led to failure once, and they will lead to failure every single time they're brought to life by an unwitting actor. They are behaviors that are so fundamentally at odds with the way the world really works, they're leading indicators of certain disaster. They are the operating manual of what *not* to do as a salesperson or a manager.

Viewed in this light, documenting Worst Practices is a worthwhile effort. Best Practices are circumstantially good ideas that may or may not apply to your company's situation. However, Worst Practices are universally bad ideas that unquestionably apply to your situation. They provide guidance on what *not* to do under *any* circumstance.

Example: Whether or not you decide to upgrade the appliances in your kitchen before putting your house on the market (perhaps a Best Practice), never leave a dead body seated at your dinner table during the open house. No one will buy your house. And you might get arrested. Don't do it under any circumstance. Ever. It's a known Worst Practice for selling a house.

WORTH READING?

Okay, documenting Worst Practices seems like a worthwhile effort. But does this justify the penning of an entire book? Lots of valuable concepts aren't very interesting to read—that's why we have textbooks. Are Worst Practices worthwhile *and* interesting, or are they more appropriate for the college bookstore than the airport bookstore?

The American comedic actor Mel Brooks once famously said, "Tragedy is when I cut my finger. Comedy is when you fall into an open sewer and die." I think this observation nicely characterizes why someone might actually read these stories of sales force failure: One man's failure is another man's entertainment.

So while observing successes can be instructive and worthy of note, the real fun in life is when someone other than yourself falls into the open sewer ... and dies. Good, clean fun. Well, fun anyway. Sure, people will want to read it. Or at least I would. The world doesn't need more textbooks—It needs more Mel Brooks.

POTENTIALLY OFFENSIVE?

Now I had to wonder what would lead me to write a book about the failures of other people? Was I being mean-spirited or spiteful? Much to the contrary. As I mentioned before, I think sales is the best. I believe that (when done properly), it is the most valuable profession in the world. A profession that occupies over 10% of the workforce and greases the gears of the global economy.

In fact, I feel compelled to recount one of the greatest speeches I ever witnessed. I was attending a meeting of the U.S. Chamber of Congress in Washington, DC, many years ago where an award was being presented to a small business that had achieved explosive international growth. As the CEO of the company stepped onstage to receive his recognition for its remarkable global success, I sighed at the prospect of another award acceptance speech. But the words that came from this man's mouth were so unexpected that I could do nothing but stare in wonderment. He began:

> *I would like to accept this award not for myself, but for all of the salespeople in our company. They're the ones who are actually responsible for all of our success outside of the United States. I accept this for the salespeople who said goodbye to their families and got on planes going to places with names they couldn't pronounce. I accept this for the salespeople who spent weeks at a time in countries where they couldn't speak the language or identify the food. This is for the salespeople who left our country with nothing more than their passports and the conviction that our products*

were the best in the world, and then returned home with
the signed contracts that led us to receive this recogni-
tion. It's our salespeople who really deserve this award,
and it's on their behalf that I gratefully accept it.

As I listened to this executive's comments, I thought a tear
would come to my eye. Sales forces so often take the blame
for poor company performance, but they never seem to receive the credit when the needle points in the other direction.
Financial success is often credited to superior products, clever
marketing, competitive positioning, or some other strategic
decision that was made in the C-suite.

But there is only one reason that companies *actually* succeed in the marketplace. It's not any magic that happens in the
boardroom—it's the magic that happens face-to-face with
customers. It's not any single decision that is made at the corporate level—it's the thousands of decisions that are made at
the street level. The front lines. The sales force.

No, to think that my motive for writing this book is ill-
natured could not be farther from the truth. I think salespeople
are the superstars of the business world, and they *do* deserve
all the credit when a company hits its revenue target. Salespeople are awesome.

ENOUGH PAPER?

That being said, salespeople do a lot of stupid things. And
there are *a lot* of salespeople. So it's completely possible that
there's not enough paper on the planet to document all of the
insane behaviors that salespeople demonstrate on a daily basis. It's just simple math.

But we will start with only twenty gems that I jotted down on bar napkins around the globe as I pondered the contents of this book. If it turns out that this collection of Worst Practices is received with a good degree of interest, then rest assured there are many more jewels where these came from. And more being created every day. Indeed, we will run out of paper before we run out of sales insanity.

YOUR GUIDE TO READING *SALES INSANITY*

The remainder of this book is an assortment of Worst Practices that I either observed or participated in myself. They are organized into two sections: one with the insane behaviors of frontline salespeople; and the other with the exceedingly poor decisions of sales leaders. Regardless of your role in the sales force, I'm confident that you'll want to read both.

The first section should be painful for almost anyone to read, because we've either committed these sins ourselves as salespeople, or we've been on the receiving end of them as customers. These stories of failure come down to errors in judgment that led to bad, bad behaviors at the point of contact with customers. And predictably, those led to bad results for the sellers.

The second section will probably be less uncomfortable on a personal level, but the behaviors are no less insane. The shock in these stories of failure is that they did not result from bad decisions made in the heat of the moment. These were premeditated, carefully considered errors that became stated strategies for entire organizations to follow. Rather than ruining a single customer interaction, these decisions created systemic failures across the entire sales force.

This is not to say that the purveyors of these bad behaviors were necessarily insane individuals. In fact, there were often completely logical reasons that led them to the brink of insanity. There was just an incorrect assumption imbedded somewhere in the logic. Or perhaps there were environmental constraints that brought on their bouts with insanity. No matter how it came about, the Worst Practice is ugly, and it inescapably leads to failure. In the following pages, these failures lead to lost sales, lost customers, or even lost companies.

It's also worth noting that all of these stories are absolutely true. In fact, they are retold pretty much as they happened and without exaggeration. As you read them, you might find yourself questioning how intelligent people could behave in such ways. Believe me, they did. And the events were perhaps even more alarming in real life than they will appear in writing. As they say, fact can be stranger than fiction.

And now, on to the stories. Let the madness begin.

PART II
SALES PERSON
INSANITY

CHAPTER THREE

A FAST PLANE TO NOWHERE

*I thought I would begin my vignettes of deviant sales be-
havior by recounting one of my own very special moments of
insanity. Like most of the salespeople mentioned in this book,
I actually do know what I am doing. Or at least, I know what I
should be doing. But also like the others in this book, there
are moments when good judgment evades me.*

THE CONTEXT

One of the craziest things about sales forces is the absolute
urgency with which they conduct their business. There is no
place in an organization where you will witness as much panic
as in sales, and this is very much by design. Daily call reports,
weekly meetings, monthly quotas, quarterly targets, frequent
incentives. … The signals to the sales force are very clear:
"Hurry, hurry, hurry. Unless you're working as fast as possible, you're not going to make it! And we're watching you!"

This forced urgency is no doubt leftover from an older age of selling. A time when harder work might actually have meant better results. When you're carrying a vacuum cleaner down the street and knocking on doors, the more doors you knock, the more vacuums you're likely to sell. This is the basic math of a transactional sales model in which the customer interactions are

> *The signals to the sales force are very clear: "Hurry, hurry, hurry!"*

all very similar and the chances of success are pretty much the same. More calls equal more sales. Hurry, hurry, hurry.

But the selling environment today is different. Sales cycles are longer. There are more stakeholders involved. The politics are complex. Buyers are sophisticated. Competition is intense. Today's professional sellers don't necessarily succeed because they make ten extra calls a day. They might actually succeed if they make ten *fewer* calls. It's all about the quality of the sales effort, not the quantity. The key message for sales forces today should be different: "Work smarter, not harder."

So what does that mean for salespeople? It means that they need to slow down and think. Slow down and plan. But planning does not come naturally for most salespeople. The only type of planning that I see routinely and voluntarily employed by salespeople is the planning of their travel schedule. Where will they be on this day? Who will they see on that trip? Will they need a plane, a train, or an automobile to get them there?

This type of planning, though, doesn't count as working smarter not harder. The type of planning that is most needed in today's selling environment is not logistical in nature—it is strategic. Sellers need to stop and ask, "What am I going to try to accomplish in this visit? Which questions should I ask? How do I expect them to respond? What will I do if things don't go as expected?" Or stop to ask: "What should be my objectives for this particular customer over the next 12 to 24 months? How will I help him accomplish *his* goals? What do I need to do differently? How will I measure my progress?"

This type of deliberation leads to smarter selling. It leads to better customer interactions. It leads to longer-term value creation. It takes selling out of the immediate and puts it into the future. But, it requires salespeople and their managers to put the important ahead of the urgent. Not hurry, hurry, hurry … rather think, think, think. In fact, it is sometimes better to do *nothing* than to do something without prior planning. Unless you're carrying a vacuum cleaner down a very long street.

THE WORST PRACTICE

I've never sold vacuum cleaners to homeowners, I have sold big projects to big companies. I have never closed a sale in a single customer interaction, and I have rarely made a sale that didn't involve many stakeholders with varying personal agendas. And I don't have an endless number of doors to knock on: there are only so many big companies that would buy my services. In other words, each opportunity is precious. Handle with care.

If there were ever a selling environment where the mandate should be to work smarter not harder, this would be it. If there were ever an environment in which planning each customer interaction is critical to success, then this is it. And I'm the professional sales consultant. I know what I should do.

However, it would seem that I am no more immune to temporary insanity than anyone else.

Last year I was pursuing a piece of consulting work with a large industrial supply company. I had worked briefly with the company a few years earlier and knew the two primary buyers reasonably well. They had called me as soon as they recognized their need for a new sales force development program, and I had subsequently worked with them to design an approach that would get them where they needed to go. I'd been selling to them for several months, and I had received very positive feedback all along. Generally, I had done a good job managing the opportunity, and I thought I was in position to win the project.

The prospect eventually narrowed the field to one other company and me. Thus began the final steps in a fairly intense dance. We were in constant communication as their deadline to make a decision approached. Phones were ringing, documents were flying, heads were nodding, and then ... silence. A complete, ahem, vacuum of communication. Like every other salesperson in the history of sales who has ever encountered this situation, the unexpected silence was very unnerving.

Their deadline passed without a sound. Then suddenly, about a week after their original date for making a decision, they called me while I was on an anniversary vacation with my wife. They were 75% certain who they were going to choose as their partner, but they had just a few more questions they wanted to run by me. Not wanting to lose this deal for lack of effort, I proposed that we meet in their offices that Monday morning to review my final proposal and to work through any remaining details.

Of course, since I was on vacation and had not intended to be in their offices Monday morning, there were all kinds of elaborate logistics to be planned. The only way to meet them on Monday morning was to take a 6:00 a.m. flight from an airport about 90 minutes from my house. Unfortunately, I did not arrive home with my wife until late Sunday afternoon. No time to waste. I speedily hugged the kids, kissed my wife, petted the dog, packed a suitcase, and headed to the airport for my early-morning flight. Then I was off to the Midwest for the do-or-die meeting with my biggest and most promising prospect at the time.

I was pleasantly surprised Monday morning when everything went according to plan ... at least, according to my travel plans. My plane was on time, and my cab zipped me to the prospect's headquarters with more than 30 minutes to spare. I signed in with reception, grabbed a visitor's badge, and took up residence in a nearby conference room. Whew. I had made it. Everything was going to be okay. Or was it?

Remarkably, it wasn't until I actually walked into the meeting that I realized how wrong things really were. For all of my immense effort and expense to get to this meeting, I had not taken the time to plan for the sales call. Not even a second. Did I have an agenda? No (even though I was the one who had requested the meeting). A proposal to review with them? No. Questions to ask? Nope. Anticipated objections to handle? Nada. I had nothing more than myself, a suitcase, and a blank stare on my face. I truly felt insane.

If I had only thought of it while riding in the cab from the airport, I could have cobbled together a framework for the meeting. But I was talking on the phone, sending e-mails, and responding to what seemed like other more urgent matters. If I had only thought of it as I was standing at the receptionist's desk, I could have asked her to print my proposal or even an agenda. But I didn't ... I was too busy speaking to another prospect by phone.

I would like to report that the meeting went well despite my lack of preparation, but it did not. I got what I deserved. I asked a series of useless questions that did little more than recount our previous conversations. They asked completely unexpected questions, that in hindsight I probably could have anticipated. The meeting ended awkwardly with neither side seeming to understand precisely why we had chosen to meet face-to-face in the first place. A total disaster.

I will never know whether I was 75% or 25% of the way to winning that deal before I ruined it with my negligent sales hygiene. All I know for sure is that my bank account is significantly lighter than it would have been if I had won that project. Regardless, I choose to believe that I lost the deal solely because of that slapdash meeting, just to keep me motivated to never let it happen again. Though I'm sure that it will. Alas, that is the nature of sales insanity.

THE GOOD IDEAS

GOOD IDEA 1: SLOW DOWN

Salespeople operate at an abnormally frenetic pace. Even if it's not in their blood, it's in their environment. Daily call reports. Weekly conference calls. Monthly quotas. It's all there to make the sales force work harder. But selling is no longer about being the fastest runner—it's about running the smartest race. If you're running too fast, you will overshoot your target. Slow down. Slow. Down.

GOOD IDEA 2: THINK

Sales is not the same as it used to be. Persuasion has been replaced with collaboration. Speed has been replaced with agility. Strength has been replaced with strategy. The salespeople who are winning today are thinkers. They are deliberate. They don't try to emulate their last successful sales call—they try to predict what will make the next one a success. Most of the salespeople I've met are smart enough to win any deal, but far fewer actually do it with any consistency. Those who do, think.

GOOD IDEA 3: PLAN

The value of planning cannot be overstated, but it's an admittedly tedious affair. Not many people enjoy doing it, but most who do will agree that it leads to better outcomes. Whether they are planning to make a sales call or to attain some other objective, the best salespeople plan. The effort that it takes is *far* outweighed by the confidence and capability it instills in them. Knowing what to do is very powerful. So slow down, think, and plan.

CHAPTER FOUR

GOT BACKBONE?

THE CONTEXT

I have often found that the skill of negotiation is a particular challenge for salespeople. Perhaps it's a challenge for people in other roles as well, but it seems somehow more pronounced in the sales force. This observation is even more befuddling when you consider that salespeople probably do more negotiating than workers in any other profession. Indeed, sales should be the domain where we find the most advanced and sophisticated negotiators ... but we don't.

One reason for this, I believe, is that the ability to negotiate well is not innate. It's a discipline with its own special skill set, particularly when the negotiations are prolonged and complex with many parties involved. Yet I've seen few sales forces that have been formally trained in the art and science of negotiation. This typically leads to two common behaviors that cost the sellers dearly.

First, the negotiations almost always take place on price, without due consideration to other elements that could be negotiated in the deal. There are many places that buyers can find value in a product or service—delivery times, payment terms, post-sales support, and such—so there should be at least as many ways to reach an agreement. However, negotiations most often are battled in a zero-sum-gain fashion. What one person gets, the other person loses.

Second, the final price is almost always closer to the buyer's opening offer than the seller's. I assume that this is the result of a perceived imbalance in power between the buyer and the seller, particularly as the deal nears an end and the final signature is in sight. For whatever reason, salespeople's backbones tend to soften progressively as the buyer's pen gets closer to a signed contract. Eventually the seller is lying limp on the floor with the buyer standing triumphantly above. The seller's price always succumbs to the law of gravity.

Regardless, most of the salespeople that I've observed will not win any awards for standing their ground. When their customers begin to push, it's as if they are wearing snow skis—gliding in reverse until they approach the cliff of zero profitability. But of all the professional skiers I've ever seen, there's one gentleman that stands out as the greatest of them all. A legend in my mind. And though the negotiation took place in a training session rather than a live customer interaction, it was so incredibly comical that I still laugh every time it comes to mind.

> *For whatever reason, salespeople's backbones tend to soften progressively as the buyer's pen gets closer to a signed contract*

THE WORST PRACTICE

I was working with a manufacturer that was trying desperately to improve its profitability in a totally flat market. After
studying their business and the economic environment, it became apparent that their ability to drive incremental volume in
the near-term was limited. Their only path to profitability was
to increase profit margin on the products that they sold. That
is, they needed to raise their prices. Or, stated more accurate-
ly, they needed to limit the size of the discounts off list price
that they were negotiating with their customers.

The difficulty here was primarily cultural. The business
had been run with a 'volume' mentality for many, many years.
Any business was good business in their minds, as long as
products moved out the door. With very few restrictions,
salespeople were allowed to discount their prices to whatever
level it took to get the deal. And the bigger the deal, the bigger the discount. So, effectively, the more volume they sold,
the more money they lost.

To further complicate the issue, the salespeople were so in-
timidated by their customers that I commented at the time that
they behaved like abused puppies. From their perspective, the
buyers held all the power, and their only form of defense was
to lower their prices at the customer's whim. To make matters
worse, their competitors' salespeople were just as afraid,
which only emboldened the customers and made the buyer-
seller relationship more difficult to manage. The salespeople
faced an uphill battle.

We therefore designed a training program for the sales
force that included, among other things, pricing and negotiating strategies. At the training event, we provided them with
some education in a classroom setting and then let them practice their new skills by participating in role plays with their

peers. The role plays were fairly straightforward—one person playing the seller and one playing the buyer. The scenario was that the salesperson had just provided a quote to a hypothetical customer, and the customer had requested a meeting to discuss the bid.

To prepare the salespeople for the role play, we broke them into two groups—those who would play the role of the buyer and those who would play the role of the seller. The sellers went to one room and planned for the 'sell side' of the interaction. They discussed their history with this particular buyer, the opening bid they had given them, what they thought the buyer's negotiating strategy might be, which questions they would ask, what non-price components they could negotiate, and what would be their 'walkaway' price (the price below which they would walk away from the deal, rather than make a money-losing sale).

I took the would-be buyers into a different room to help them plan for the 'buy side' of the call. We discussed their business needs, the bid they had received from the seller, the bids they had received from competitors, the points they wanted to negotiate, and their desired outcomes for the call. Pretty basic stuff. Except that the buyers in this role play were told to not go for the low-price jugular. They were told to emphasize other things that were more important to their business, like delivery times and credit terms. Just like real customers. Time to negotiate.

It just so happened that there were not enough salespeople to fill up the training class, so the event coordinator had invited an administrator from the local office to participate in the meeting. The young woman pulled me aside as we were breaking out of our planning session and asked if she could opt out of the role play. She explained quite earnestly that she was extremely shy and very uncomfortable with confrontational situations. I told her she had to do the role play, but she didn't need to be combative. She simply needed to get the conversation started, and then the seller would take the lead. She asked, "Well, what should I say to get the conversation started?" As we were walking into the room to begin the role play, I offhandedly responded, "Just tell him that his price is too high." She nodded.

The three of us sat down at the table: the young woman as the fictitious buyer, a young salesperson as the seller, and me as the observer. The shy administrator held a sheet of paper in her hand with the seller's original bid, slumped her shoulders as if she wanted to melt into her chair, and stared directly at the table, making no eye contact whatsoever with the seller.

Seller: Hi, Kate. It's good to see you again. I understand from your voicemail message that you'd like to discuss the bid that we gave you for the upcoming project in Philadelphia. What is it that you wanted to talk about?

Sheepish Buyer (still staring at the table): Well [very long silence] … Your price is too high.

Well-Coached Seller (trying to build benefits rather than discount price): Hmm. Well, I want you to feel like you're getting the most value for your money here. First, let's talk about the delivery schedule. Since our warehouse is 50 miles closer to this job than our nearest competitor, we can guarantee you that our trucks will be on-site by 7:00 a. m. You've mentioned before that timely delivery is important to you. Is that still the case?

Buyer: Well, umm … Your price is too high. [longer, more uncomfortable silence]

Concerned Seller (the sales call is not going according to plan): Well, Kate, we're also offering you some pretty flexible payment terms, which you've taken advantage of in the past. Is that something we could talk about here?

Buyer (still staring at the table, wanting to disappear): Well [even longer, more uncomfortable silence] ... Your price is too high.

Unnerved Seller (transforming into abused puppy): Okay. You say that the price is too high. I understand that. What are the specific items on the list that you think are priced too high? Let's look at them each individually.

Buyer: I guess all of it. I don't know. Your price is just too high.

At this point, the buyer's job was done. The seller totally collapsed. The young salesperson leaned forward, took a pen from his pocket, and went through all 15 items on the bid one at a time, marking each price down as low as he could possibly imagine. During this self-inflicted, frenetic exercise in discounting, the seller did not utter a single word. It was a one-man mark-down fiesta. In the end, he took a bid that was originally priced at $22,000 and transformed it into a money-losing masterpiece of around $13,000. And all the while, he was negotiating with himself—the buyer said nothing. It was just him and his presumption that he could only win the business with the lowest possible price.

But the real show had yet to begin. We then reassembled as a group to debrief the exercise and share the outcomes of the individual negotiations.

Another Facilitator on my Team: First, let's get all the numbers up here on the board and see how the negotiations turned out. Group 1, did you reach an agreement? Okay, what was your final sale price? $20,500. Not bad. Group 2? $19,700. Okay. Group 3? $17,250 [boos from the crowd]. Group 4? $22,000 [cheers from the crowd]. Great job on that. We'll come back to you in a minute to see how you got full price. Group 5 (my group)? $13,000? Did you say $13,000?

Crowd: What the ...? [All heads turn.] How on earth did you get beaten down to $13,000? Who were you negotiating against?

Abused Puppy: Kate.

Crowd: Kate?! Kate?! Kate negotiated you out of $9,000?! [Cheers for Kate, who is slightly smiling for the first time.] Dude, Kate crushed you!

Facilitator: Okay, let's start with you then, Group 5. Going into the negotiation, what was your walkaway price?

Abused Puppy: $17,500

Facilitator: $17,500? And you settled at $13,000? How did you get so far below your walkaway price?

(No response. Total silence, except for the heckling from nearby tables.)

Facilitator: Kate, What was your strategy going into this negotiation?

Kate: I dunno. I didn't really have one.

Facilitator: Then how did you negotiate his price so low?

Kate: I didn't really. I just told him that his price was too high, and he lowered it. I didn't really do anything. I don't know.

At this point, the seller had assumed Kate's earlier disposition, staring at the table with defeated shoulders. As I watched this unfold, I knew with certainty that this same negotiation had no doubt taken place in many previous interactions with this salesperson's customers. And though he had certainly lost gobs of money for his company in the past, this was exponentially worse for him—public humiliation in front of his peers. Devastating. He later told me it had been a "life-altering event." In fact, I sometimes wonder if he now has the strongest backbone of anyone in that sales force. A good lesson, learned the hard way.

THE GOOD IDEAS

GOOD IDEA 1: NEGOTIATING SKILL IS INVALUABLE FOR A SALESPERSON

Generally speaking, there's not enough education or training for salespeople on the skill of negotiating. Unfortunately, negotiating is far down the training agenda behind product knowledge, information systems, and other more tactical things. However, this skill is so critical that salespeople should seek training themselves if necessary. The ability to negotiate goes beyond just defending your price—it is foundational to developing and demonstrating a value-added relationship with your customer.

GOOD IDEA 2: PRICE IS ONLY ONE OF MANY SOURCES OF VALUE

Simply seeing the word 'negotiate' takes most people's minds immediately to 'price.' However, the price is typically only one component of a larger value proposition. When you find yourself in a negotiation, be sure to get all the sources of value on the table. Make certain that the customer knows what else you have to offer—what other benefits do they stand to receive? If the negotiation takes place solely on price, you have done a disservice to both yourself and to your customer.

GOOD IDEA 3: HAVE A BACKBONE

No explanation required.

CHAPTER FIVE

I RECEIVED A REQUEST FOR PROPOSAL!

THE CONTEXT

Most salespeople are taught early in their careers the importance of qualifying new leads. A qualified lead stands a good chance of being won, but an unqualified lead can cost you days, months, or even years of wasted effort. So when you determine a lead is qualified, you should pursue it like a pot of gold. But when you find that a lead is *un*qualified, you should immediately drop it like an angry skunk. Taking the time to assess the quality of a new lead is critical to being an effective and efficient seller.

Furthermore, salespeople are given fairly universal criteria to determine whether or not a lead is qualified enough to pursue. Foremost, the prospective buyer must have a clearly articulated *need*. Unless the buyer's need is known, it's not only uncertain that she'll find a solution, it's even less certain that you'll have the product she'll want to buy.

Second, a qualified lead must have *timeline*. Even if a prospect knows what she needs, a sales cycle could go on forever without a definitive date on the calendar for the customer to make the actual purchase.

Third, the purchase must have an allocated *budget*. If the purchasing company hasn't yet committed any funds to solving their need, then how serious can it really be? But more importantly, how seriously should the seller want to pursue it?

Finally, the *buying process* and its participants must be defined. Even if a buyer has the budget to solve a need on a short timeline, it's an unqualified lead until the wheels are put in motion to actually make a purchase.

So sellers are taught early and often that an opportunity is 'qualified' and worthy of pursuit if there is a clear need, a budget, a timeline, and a buying process. And this all makes sense. If each of those conditions is met, then someone is almost certain to buy something from someone. It then becomes the seller's job to make sure the customer buys it from him. Enter the Request for Proposal.

A Request for Proposal, or RFP, is a document issued by a purchasing company to a select group of 'vendors' that it believes can meet its stated purchasing criteria. Frequently the document outlines those purchasing criteria and requests that interested vendors respond to the RFP with a proposal to meet the buyer's needs. And boy, are vendors interested to respond.

On the surface, an RFP appears to be a perfectly qualified lead. There is a clearly defined need—in fact, it's typically described in great detail within the document. And the timeline is also commonly stated in the RFP, with purchasing milestones laid out from the deadline for responses to the date the winning vendor will be announced.

And though the prospective buyers will rarely reveal their budget in an RFP, it's assumed that the company has committed resources to the purchase, because the issuance of the document itself requires an investment of organizational effort. If they've written an RFP, there's probably a budget somewhere.

The buying process can be opaque in an RFP, because the buyers don't want to reveal who has the ultimate decision-making authority (if they even know). But again, it's assumed that a purchasing company has an internally defined process, or else they wouldn't have been able to

> *On the surface, a Request for Proposal appears to be a perfectly qualified lead*

reach consensus on all the conditions above. So does an RFP then represent a highly qualified lead? It would seem to check all the boxes.

Often sellers receive an RFP after months of diligent work trying to position themselves to participate in the pending opportunity. But sometimes RFPs just show up in their inbox—a totally unexpected gift that no one saw coming. These invitations can seem like blessings from above, but in my experience there's just one problem when a salesperson receives an unanticipated RFP: it's almost always unwinnable.

Sure, there are certain industries where an RFP process is the way that purchasing necessarily gets done—most notably government purchasers who are required to go through the exercise to assure the prudent use of taxpayers' money. But most RFPs are not issued out of legal compliance. They are issued because the formality of the process provides the patina of an objective purchasing decision. However, RFP processes are rarely objective purchasing decisions.

By the time the Request for Proposals is issued, a lot of effort has already been put into exploring solutions in the marketplace, and a lot of conversations have already been had with potential solution providers. If there isn't already a leading contender to win the business, the criteria in the RFP have certainly been influenced by vendors that were engaged with the buyers before you were ceremoniously invited to participate.

When you receive an RFP that you didn't know was coming, the chances are that you've already lost. BUT it will look like a highly qualified lead that is worthy of an immediate and fevered response, because it is highly qualified according to the previous criteria. There's a need, a budget, a timeline, and a buying process. Someone is certain to buy something from someone—it just won't be from you.

THE WORST PRACTICE

I could recount the many, many times that colleagues and I have jumped with excitement when an RFP unexpectedly appeared. I could count all of the hours we've spent hurriedly assembling a team to write a proposal that would assuredly bring us windfall revenue from a 'bluebird' deal. But I won't.

Instead, I thought it would be interesting to recount a story from the opposite perspective—the perspective of the winner who was invisibly conspiring with the buyer to get the business *before* the RFP was ever written. Well, we were actually conspiring inadvertently, but conspiring nonetheless.

I received a call one day from the head of sales at a large manufacturer. He had read something I'd published online and was interested to learn if my company could help him define a sales strategy for his team. More specifically, he wanted to define a sales process for his sales team to launch a new product into the marketplace. Could we help him? Of course we could.

Over the next several weeks, we defined the scope of work and assembled a project plan to help his sales force do exactly that. Everything was on path for a nice consulting engagement—we even had resources assigned to the effort and a kick-off date selected. But in a classic example of bad timing, the sales force's parent company announced bad quarterly financial results, and all discretionary spending was frozen. Within days of beginning work, the project was pronounced dead.

Almost two years later, I received a call from the same head of sales who told me that he still wanted to do the project, and he once more had the funding in place to proceed. The project was alive! We quickly dusted off the original project plan, assembled a team of consultants, and selected another kick-off date for the newly revived gig.

As we were arranging travel to the company's headquarters to meet the client's project team, I received an alarming call from the head of sales. He'd been informed by his boss that the project would have to be put 'out to bid' to at least two other vendors, since the total cost of the effort exceeded a half-million dollars. My stomach fell to the floor.

Hearing that we'd been put into a competitive battle for this previously assured project, I immediately asked if a vendor-selection committee had been formed. He said it had. I then asked how soon I could fly to his office to meet the other decision-makers. In my mind, I had over two years invested in this sale. I was determined to not lose this work to a competitor.

"No need to worry," said the head of sales. "We're still going to do this project with you."

"But if you're going to issue an RFP for this project, I need to meet the other decision-makers and start building relationships with them," I responded, while trying to mask my growing panic.

"Seriously, don't worry about this. Just sit tight. Give me two weeks, and then we'll pick up where we left off."

As promised, we were back on the telephone two weeks later re-scheduling the project kick-off meeting.

"So what happened during these last two weeks?" I asked.

"I had to get some quotes from other consulting firms. No big deal," he replied.

"So you issued an RFP and got proposals from two other consulting firms in just two weeks?"

"It was three other firms, actually. And yes, we got proposals from all of them."

"So dare I ask if we were the lowest bidder?"

[Audible laughter.] "Not even close. But you're the company we were going to do this with regardless. It was your project. I just had to jump through some hoops to make it work internally."

And that was that.

I've often looked back at that two-week period and chuckled to myself. While I was 'sitting tight' awaiting my client's go-ahead call, three other consulting firms were entered in an imaginary contest to win an unwinnable project. They must have danced their RFP jig and assembled teams of people to quickly respond with a winning proposal. A new lead with a defined need, timeline, budget, and buying process had unexpectedly landed on their desks. The project was probably put into their sales pipeline, and their forecasts were probably updated. Someone was going to win that project for sure. It just wasn't going to be them.

THE GOOD IDEAS

GOOD IDEA 1: VIEW UNANTICIPATED RFPS WITH SKEPTICISM

RFPs look like highly qualified leads, and sometimes they are. But in my experience, most times they are not. When an RFP lands in your lap, try to talk yourself out of responding to it rather than automatically assuming that you will. Really look at it with a skeptical eye. If the description of the buyer's need looks like it could have been written by a competitor, then it probably was. If the timeline seems unrealistic, then it probably is. If you don't think you are the perfect vendor to provide this work, then you probably aren't. Don't assume the best when you receive an RFP: assume the worst.

GOOD IDEA 2: A LEAD IS NOT QUALIFIED UNLESS YOU CAN WIN IT

Classic qualification criteria for a 'good' lead are meant to ensure that the buyer is ready to spend her money. If they have a need, a budget, a timeline, and a buying process, then the stage is set for a successful purchase. But NOT necessarily for a successful sale. If the deal is unwinnable, then it's not really qualified. The buyer might be ready to buy, but that doesn't mean he's ready to buy from you. Don't let the excitement of an inevitable purchase fool you into believing that it's your inevitable sale.

CHAPTER SIX

LOOK HOW VALUABLE WE ARE TO YOU

THE CONTEXT

Different companies have different revenue models, and each has its own unique challenges. For instance, most management consultants generate revenue by selling their time. And that time is typically spent working on a clearly defined project, with a discrete beginning and a discrete end. So if you hire me to help you design an incentive compensation plan for your sales team, I might work on that project for several weeks and then move on to another project with another client. I sell my time in chunks.

In this revenue model, the challenge is to continually find new projects. Consultants need to sell project after project to maintain a steady stream of revenue, because each project is a stand-alone piece of business. And there are many companies that face a similar challenge of having to constantly find new customers. In fact, most companies rely on new customer acquisition. If they don't acquire new customers, their companies will die.

But some companies have revenue models that are less reliant on a steady stream of new customers. They are fortunate enough to have streams of 'recurring' revenue that just flow and flow from a base of existing customers. You can think of these as subscription services in one form or another, like your phone company, your bank, or even your family dentist. They provide you with a service that you find valuable, and you repay that value with your loyalty and an ongoing string of payments. As long as you remain happy with the service they provide, they enjoy predictable revenue.

In this revenue model, the challenge is not necessarily to continually find new customers, though that's certainly a path to growth. In this situation, the most important goal of all is to retain your existing customers. Or at least it should be. Study after study has shown that it's much more profitable to retain an existing customer than to acquire a new one. But you don't need a researcher to tell you that—it just makes sense.

However, I can't begin to count the number of companies I've seen that ignore this obvious fact. The appeal of signing up new customers is so great that they put their very best sellers on the hunt for fresh faces, and they architect their sales forces to promote and reward the acquisition of new customers. In these companies, nothing—and I mean *nothing*—is as celebrated as bringing in a new customer.

Not surprisingly, these companies often end up with a trickle of new buyers coming in the front door, while a river of existing customers gushes out the back. They fail to appreciate the real source of their financial well-being. It's not necessarily a growing number of new customers, but a *happy* base of existing customers.

Keeping customers happy is not an unsolvable mystery. You just have to demonstrate enough value that they keep coming back. Every time a customer makes a payment to such a 'subscription,' she does the math in her head. *Is this service still worth the price that I'm paying?* If yes, then your steady stream of revenue keeps right on coming. If the answer is no, then she will jump into the gushing river and ride it out your back door.

> *Nothing is as celebrated as bringing in a new customer*

THE WORST PRACTICE

The irony in this next installment of sales insanity is so thick that I hardly know how to begin the story. By now you know my distaste for the Best Practice. Well, there are several organizations that do nothing but conduct ongoing research to identify emerging Best Practices. They then sell these 'insights' to their customers who attempt to implement the Current Best Practices in their own companies. These research firms have been very successful, and most large companies pay them for their insights.

The revenue model for these firms is subscription based, so their customers write large checks each year to extend their access to the databases of research. In theory, there's enough valuable new research conducted every year to justify the customer's annual investment and keep the checks coming. But like any subscription service, if the customer doesn't see the value, then the checks don't get sent.

Since these firms do nothing but identify Best Practices, you would expect these organizations to be brilliantly managed with highly competent sales forces. You would expect their salespeople to be experts in their field and to demonstrate Best Practice skills when developing and nurturing customer relationships. You would expect their annual renewals to be well-orchestrated exercises where their salespeople are equipped to demonstrate the value that their research provides. And you would be wrong.

One day I was sitting in the office the SVP of sales and marketing for a large global manufacturer. The company's director of sales operations happened to stroll by and comment that their annual subscription for one of these Best Practices research firms was up for renewal. Playing the role of troublemaker, I asked, "Are you sure you're getting a lot of value out of that subscription? It seems kind of expensive, given some of the other priorities that I know you have for the upcoming year."

"That's a good question," the SVP replied, and he asked his colleague to look into it. The director of sales operations, being a deliberate and thorough person, immediately contacted the research firm's salesperson who was assigned to the manufacturing company. He asked the salesperson to provide him with a report of the following:

- A list of all the people from the manufacturing company who had logged into the Best Practices database during the previous 12 months;
- The number of times documents had been downloaded from the database;
- A description of each document that had been downloaded and the person who had requested it.

Now, any sane salesperson would have understood exactly what was happening here. The director of sales operations was clearly requesting this information for only one purpose—to determine whether or not the subscription was providing enough value to be renewed for another 12 months. And you would have expected this salesperson to have known what was at stake: demonstrate value or else watch the customer drop into the gushing river of lost revenue. You'd have expected the seller to be as thorough as the buyer and to handle the situation with some sense of anxiety and attention to detail. And again, you'd be wrong.

The seller responded to the director's request with an e-mail attachment and nothing more. No phone call. No text in the e-mail asking about the nature of the request. And most damaging, no commentary about the contents of the attached report that was about to set in motion the manufacturing company's decision to cancel its annual subscription.

The report revealed that only one employee had logged into the database of Best Practices during the previous 12 months. One. And that person was no longer employed by the manufacturer; he had left to work for a competitor several months earlier. So, literally, no one currently working at the company had logged into the service since its last renewal.

To make the story worse (or better), this former employee had logged into the database exactly twice before leaving the company, and he had downloaded research on two diverse topics. The first topic was the competitor's company where the employee eventually went to work. Yes, he had used the expensive database of Best Practices to do research for his job interviews with another prospective employer. In this case, the subscription service might actually have created a *negative* return on the investment, since it led to increased employee turnover.

But the second topic the former employee had researched was much more comical. He had used the database to research baby food. Apparently, the gentleman had recently become a father, and he was somehow able to use a database of business Best Practices to unearth data on the quality of several brands of baby formula. This was perhaps more useful and well-intentioned than doing research for a job interview, but still not the intended use of the expensive subscription service.

As you might expect, this subscription was immediately cancelled. In my mind, I like to imagine the disappointment and feeling of betrayal that the salesperson might have felt when notified of the lost customer. I also like to image that the seller never came to know the reason for the cancellation. I like to think he unwittingly forwarded this ridiculous information without even reading the report. Either way, it's insane behavior.

If the seller *didn't* know what was in the report, then that is even worse. It was negligent selling—sales malpractice of the highest order. If the seller *did* know what was in the report, then that demonstrated either an unfathomable level of arrogance or an unfathomable level of apathy. Also insane behaviors. And certainly not Best Practice selling—from a company that sells Best Practices. As I said, the irony is thick.

In fairness, it would have been tough for the salesperson to convince the manufacturer that the database had created much value that year because it simply hadn't been used. But perhaps he could have pulled forward usage data from previous years that could have made the case for renewal. Or perhaps he could have uncovered some future business need that would have justified keeping the service. Alas, we will never know. All we have is an entertaining story to share.

THE GOOD IDEAS

GOOD IDEA 1: RETAINING EXISTING CUSTOMERS IS MORE FUN THAN YOU THINK

In sales, we *love* to acquire new customers. A 'hunter' who brings in new business it typically praised much more loudly than a 'farmer' who retains and grows existing accounts. But make no mistake, if you're throwing parties at the front door and quietly losing customers out the back, you are doing yourself a grave disservice. It's easier to keep a customer than to win one, so don't let the good ones wash away.

GOOD IDEA 2: DEMONSTRATE VALUE OR ELSE LOSE YOUR CUSTOMERS

Many sales forces have revenue models where prolonged customer satisfaction is somewhat irrelevant. They sell a stand-alone product to one customer and move on to the next. The fortunes of other sales forces are very closely tied to their customers' perception of value. If you rely on repeat customers for your livelihood, then you *must* demonstrate value *before* the next purchase decision. Otherwise, you'll be fighting a losing battle, because history will not be on your side.

GOOD IDEA 3: PAY ATTENTION TO THE DETAILS

Salespeople live in a chaotic, hurried environment. There's never enough time to complete all of their tasks, and any opportunity to take a shortcut can appear like a great idea. But usually it's not. Even the smallest oversights can have expensive and long-lasting consequences. If you're one of those people who likes to use the "Replace All" function in your word processor, then sales might be a dangerous career for you. When customers are involved, the details matter. A lot.

CHAPTER SEVEN

IT'S THE 'MARKET PRICE'

THE CONTEXT

Sales forces are obsessed with revenue. In fact, most measures of success inside a sales force are quantified in terms of revenue. Salespeople's quotas are set in terms of revenue. Their sales pipelines are denominated in revenue. Sales forecasts are based in revenue. Commissions are calculated off revenue. Everywhere you look in a sales force, you see revenue, revenue, revenue.

However, revenue is the most generalized measure of success. It's the number that is the simplest to quantify and the easiest to discuss, but it's not the ultimate goal of a company. In reality, profit is what determines whether or not a company's doors stay open and its lights stay on. It's the *bottom* line that determines how healthy a company really is, not the more blunt top line. Revenue is great, but profit is the best.

Yet we don't talk about profitability very much inside the sales force. No salesperson I know has a profit quota. Or a profit pipeline. Or a profit forecast. A handful of sellers I've seen in my career were compensated based on profitability, but a small handful. As a rule, all sales forces are managed using this topline metric of revenue, and it will almost certainly remain that way until the end of time.

Of course, there are good reasons for this phenomenon. Foremost, many salespeople don't have control over the profitability of the products and services they sell. Prices are set by another entity inside their companies—most often the marketing department. Profitability is predetermined in these cases, and the goal of the salespeople is rightfully to just sell as much stuff as possible. The more revenue the sellers generate, the more profit their company reaps.

But in other situations, salespeople have a great deal of control over the profitability of what they sell. They have the power to configure the products and services that they offer to their customers, and they have the ability to negotiate price. These salespeople not only influence the cost of what they sell, they determine the profit margin as well.

In this situation, things can get dicey. Recall that these salespeople are not compensated on profitability—they are compensated based on the revenue they produce. Consequently, the economic incentives of the sellers and their employers are not necessarily aligned, and company profits often evaporate.

Imagine that I'm a salesperson who sells a product with a $10 list price and a $1 profit margin. If I let a customer negotiate my price down to $8.50, then my company is now losing 50¢ on the product I just sold.

> *The economic incentives of sellers and their employers are not necessarily aligned, and company profits often evaporate*

However, I get paid a commission on $8.50 of revenue. In other words, I lost 15% of my commission, but my company lost all of its profit. Plus 50¢. Not a good deal for the company.

But in defense of salespeople who negotiate away profit in pursuit of commissions, most of them don't even know they're doing it. They do not have clear visibility into the profit margins of the products that they sell. They're just told to go find some customers, sell them some products, and negotiate the price if they must. And that's what they do.

THE WORST PRACTICE

An industrial distributor hired me along with a team of consultants to help identify ways to increase its profitability. The company was eking out the slightest profit, but it was headed toward losses that it could not endure. Its executive team knew that there was profitability hiding somewhere in the company, because its similarly structured competitors were performing much better in the same economic environment. They were confident that the operations side of their business was running efficiently and that their missing profits could be found in the sales force. We subsequently sent our search party into the field to test their hypothesis.

We began by interviewing the company's salespeople. Among other things, we asked each seller, "Who are your very best customers?" Not surprisingly, the salespeople immediately responded with a list of their very biggest customers—the customers that generated the most revenue for the company. And from their perspective, these *were* their best customers, because they yielded the most money in commissions. The incentives of the sellers were based on achieving revenue targets, not achieving profits. Therefore, bigger was better.

We also asked the salespeople who they thought were their most profitable customers. Again, they listed their biggest customers by revenue. We asked, "Don't your big customers negotiate lower prices with you, because of the volume of products they buy?" "Of course the pricing with those customers is a little bit lower," the sellers all responded, "but the absolute dollar amounts of the profits must be high despite the lower margins." Except that they weren't.

At the same time we were conducting the interviews, we were also busy calculating the actual profitability for each of the company's customers. It turned out that in addition to negotiating lower prices, the sellers' biggest customers were also the slowest to pay their invoices. And they returned a lot of products. And they demanded the most customer service. And they received volume rebates. When all of the costs to sell and service them were taken into account, the company was making a profit on just 14 of its 50 biggest customers. It was *losing* money on 72% of its 'best' customers. That's where the company's profits were hiding.

In itself, this didn't shock me. The salespeople had no knowledge of the actual profitability of the products they were selling, and their financial incentives clearly inspired them to close any deal no matter how low the price. What did surprising to me, though, was the vehemence with which they defended their price discounting practices.

Every salesperson in the company had large customers that were sucking money out from this company. We pointed out that they were essentially *paying* these customers for the privilege of selling them products, and if they were to stop selling to 36 of their 50 biggest-volume customers, their company would actually be *more* profitable. We suggested that

they needed to raise their prices to these profit-sucking customers, or else we would be forced to fire them—their
customers, not the salespeople.

But to a person, they defended their pricing tactics as what
they had to do in order to 'get the business.' In fact, they
claimed that getting this business was the privilege they had
earned over decades by developing great personal friendships
with their customers. These customers were generous enough
to give them the 'last look' at each potential deal, so they
could beat the lowest price that their competitors had to offer.

Again, we pointed out that this was a bad strategy, but the
salespeople were steadfast that they were simply meeting the
'market price' established by their competition. If they didn't
sell the products to the customer at the 'market price,' then
their competitors would win the business. To which we responded, "Great. Let your competitors win the business. Let
them pay the customers to buy their products. Then your
competitors will be the first to go bankrupt, not you."

Alas, no amount of reasoning could convince these salespeople that selling products at a loss was a losing proposition.
They were convinced that they should continue to 'get the
business' at the 'market price' by leveraging their 'friendships' to get the 'last look' at every deal. No wonder their
competition was performing more profitably than they were.
The competitors' salespeople were smart enough to say no to
the worst deals.

Gratefully, this story had a happy ending. The executives
realized that the sales force's financial incentives were not
aligned with the company's. They cleverly redesigned the
compensation plans to reward profitable customer relationships, not just big ones. Within a year, the distributor's profits
were on the rise, and they continued to grow substantially for
several more years.

As these changes were taking place, I liked to imagine the amazed reactions of the competitors' sellers as my client's salespeople began to walk away from bad deals. The competitors must have marveled at their good fortune. Suddenly they were getting the last look at all the deals they'd previously lost to my client. They were able to win the business, and win it at the market price. Their revenues were surely on the way up. But their profitability was on the way down.

THE GOOD IDEAS

GOOD IDEA 1: BIGGER ISN'T NECESSARILY BETTER

There is an intuitive appeal to bigger customers. And all things being equal, they tend to be better for you, too. But not always. Sometimes your biggest customers might also be your worst, because they're either less profitable, less strategic, or just more annoying. Be sure to understand the type of customers you want, and then do what you can to attract and retain those. You don't need every customer, just the ones that are good for your company.

GOOD IDEA 2: BEWARE THE 'MARKET PRICE'

The 'market price' is a customer euphemism for the lowest price that anyone has ever spoken aloud. Don't lead a race to the bottom just because someone tells you a lower price exists. You shouldn't have to give away your products—they deserve a price that reflects the true value you provide to your customers. If your customers won't buy at a price that you want to sell, then politely walk away. Let 'the market' have the business instead.

GOOD IDEA 3: YOU MIGHT HAVE TO FIRE A CUSTOM-
ER

Salespeople spend most of their energy trying to acquire
and grow customers, so it's almost unthinkable to purposefully end an active customer relationship. But like any
relationship, some customers who start out as a dream will
end up a nightmare. If they're a bad customer to you, hopefully they'll be an even worse customer to your competitor. Let
them be just that.

CHAPTER EIGHT

LOOK, I'M THE EXPERT

THE CONTEXT

As a practical reality, salespeople need to know more about the products they sell than their customers do, because it helps them to add value in the sales process. Customers expect sellers to understand what's 'under the hood' of the products they sell and to connect their product's unique capabilities to the customer's specific needs. In many ways, salespeople are playing matchmaker between the particulars of their offerings and the particulars of their buyers. The better sellers understand their products, the better the match they can subsequently make.

That said, when salespeople become too obsessed with the features and functions of their products, their knowledge can weigh them down. They become so enamored with the product side of the discussion that they lose focus on the customer side. They become talking brochures that prefer to spout product details rather than focus on buyer needs.

This is especially true in industries where the products or services are very technical in nature. As a retail consumer, you've probably had sales interactions with highly technical sales reps, whether in electronics stores or car lots. Salespeople who have been well trained on their products *love* to talk about their products. Nothing is more compelling to these sellers than the technical specifications at the molecular level, while nothing is more compelling to their buyers than a hasty exit from the tedious conversation. Highly technical salespeople can simultaneously overwhelm and underwhelm buyers with their extensive product knowledge, leaving their buyers exasperated and exhausted.

Note that 'technical' salespeople aren't relegated to just high tech industries. They can be found in any industry where the details under the surface are important but are beyond the necessary understanding of the buyer. I would include professionals such as lawyers, accountants, and engineers in this group. These are people that we pay for their deep understanding of their disciplines, but we don't aspire to understand to those depths ourselves.

In fact, professionals like lawyers, accountants, and engineers face a particular sales challenge, because they are not hired as salespeople. They're hired and succeed early in their careers because they are technically proficient in their fields. Then at some point in their career progression, they are forced to become 'rainmakers' if they want to become executives in their firms.

They don't call themselves

> *Highly technical salespeople can simultaneously overwhelm and underwhelm buyers with their extensive product knowledge*

salespeople, nor are they trained as salespeople, but they're undeniably sellers. They have quotas, and their compensation is linked to the volume of client revenue they generate. Yet they remain technologists at heart. Any chance to demonstrate their knowledge of their craft is an opportunity not to be missed. And very bad selling can ensue.

THE WORST PRACTICE

I have started small businesses at several times in my career. When you start a company, there's one decision that must be made rather early in the process: Which type of tax entity best fits the business. In this area, I know only enough to know that I don't know enough. Tax laws and regulations constantly change, and there are endless complications that only an expert can appreciate. So when setting up a new business, I've always sought the counsel of a tax professional. Several years ago, I did exactly that.

I had scheduled an appointment with a tax accountant who was referred to me by a colleague. When I spoke to the gentleman on the phone, I was as direct as I could be about my expectations for our first meeting. I explained that I was searching for an accounting firm to help me set up a new company and to prepare its taxes going forward. I even told him that I was interviewing a few other accountants who had been referred to me, and I would choose only one. In other words, this was a sales call from his perspective, and his job was to sell me on his firm. I met him at his office:

Me: Hi there. It's a pleasure to meet you.

Accountant: Yes, it's a pleasure to meet you, too.

Me: As I explained during our phone conversation, I'm starting a new company, and I'd like some advice on how it should be structured from a tax perspective. I have high hopes for this company, and I hope to build a long-term relationship with the firm I choose to help me going forward.

Accountant: Great, we certainly hope that we will be that firm. Tell me a little about the new company.

Me: It will be a professional services firm, and I'll be the only owner with a few employees. I also won't have any outside investors in the company, so I feel like it might be a fairly simple situation.

Accountant: Well, it might seem simple, but it's actually very, very complex. Do you mind if I call in one of my associates to join us for this conversation?

Me: No, of course not. Please do.

[He does]

Associate: Hi, It's a pleasure to meet you.

Me: You too.

Partner (looking at his associate): We were just discussing a new business that he's starting, and I was explaining how complex his seemingly simple situation really is. (Looking at me for the last time) Could you please repeat to her what you just told me?

[I do.]

Accountant (speaking directly to his associate): So, what do you think about his situation?

Associate (speaking directly to the partner): Well, it's certainly not simple. The potential issues could be very complex.

Me: Well, I realize that the issues are probably more complex than I can appreciate. That's why I'm here. I'm hoping you can simplify them for me.

Accountant (speaking to his associate): So what do you think he should do?

Associate (speaking to partner): Well, there is the consideration of <some accounting concept I don't understand>, which could affect the tax basis of his equity. Regardless of what we choose to do, we could file a <government form I don't know> so he avoids paying <a tax I don't know>.

Accountant: But what about the possibility of forming <some other tax entity>? Would that avoid <another tax I don't know>?

Associate: Potentially, but not unless we designate his payroll as <some unknown tax designation>.

[Partner nods thoughtfully. Associate continues. Partner responds. Associate nods thoughtfully. Partner continues. Associate responds. Repeat.]

This two-person serenade of tax-code trivia continued for 25 minutes—which is a long time when you're sitting in silence unsure of what's happening around you. It was like getting pulled from a basic math classroom in high school and dropped into an advanced calculus exam. I could understand about 20% of what they were saying, but the other 80% was so confusing that it made me doubt the 20% that I already knew.

I tried several times to bring the discussion back to my original question, since there were really only three alternatives for structuring the company. But apparently the three hundred technical details underlying those three alternatives were much more important to discuss (or at least more entertaining for them). At the end of the session, the accounting partner seemed quite pleased with all that had transpired:

Accountant: So I hope you can appreciate the many complexities of your situation. I think our firm is highly qualified to help you navigate these issues and get you on the right path. Do you agree?

Me [trying to refocus my attention from the wall at which I'd begun staring blankly]: Umm. … Yes. It sounds like you all really know your stuff.

Accountant: Great, shall we schedule a follow-up meeting?

Me: If you would, please give me a chance to process all that you've discussed here, and I'll call your office in a week or two.

And I did. But not to schedule a follow-up meeting—rather it was to tell him goodbye. Forever. I instead chose an accountant who was able to explain my alternatives to me in a simple language that I could understand. Was the accountant I eventually chose a better tax technician than the one I dismissed? I don't know. Would my chosen accountant do a better job for me? I don't know that either. But I felt more comfortable and confident with the seller who made me feel like my questions had been answered, rather than the one that had dazzled me into technical submission.

This story involves a professional services firm, but I've seen this same scenario played out in the offices of dozens of my clients. From software companies to industrial manufacturers, the issue is the same: When sellers know a lot about their products, they want to show it. Whether it's the processing speed of a computer or the tensile strength of a steel beam, the details always seem more interesting and impressive to discuss than the customer's issues. Except to the customers. And that's how sales get lost.

THE GOOD IDEAS

GOOD IDEA 1: TECHNICAL DETAILS MATTER LESS TO THE BUYER

Despite the high level of technical expertise you possess as a seller, buyers care most about solving their own problems. And those problems are inevitably functional in nature, not technical. Fight the desire to share all the gory technical details until you've demonstrated that you can solve the customer's functional problem. Then perhaps the buyer will be interested enough to ask for a deeper dive into your solution.

GOOD IDEA 2: IMPRESS THE BUYER, NOT YOURSELF

It feels great to be the expert, and it feels even better to show someone else how much of an expert you are. But the buyer is the one who needs to be elevated during a sales interaction, not the seller. A sales call is not the time to impress yourself or your colleagues—it's a time to impress upon the buyer that you can relieve their pain and lead them to a better place. Buyers need experts who can *apply* their expertise, not just revel in it.

CHAPTER NINE

I KNOW WHAT MY CUSTOMERS WANT

THE CONTEXT

Every salesperson has customers. A salesperson without customers is like a flower without sunlight—it's unhappy, malnourished, and probably won't be around for long. But some salespeople have customers that are the sunlight, water, and soil of their subsistence. They are the customers that these salespeople cannot live without because they supply most, if not all, of the salesperson's revenue and resulting income.

Often salespeople are hired specifically to manage a few large customers, and they have titles like Major Account Managers or Strategic Account Reps. These salespeople may have only a few accounts assigned to them, and it's quite obvious that these special customers will be the center of each salesperson's universe. It's how their roles are defined.

But even when salespeople are hired to service 100 or 200 customers, it's not uncommon to discover that the majority of their revenue is coming from only a few large customers. Regardless of whether the title on their business cards reads

Major Account Manager, sellers can still find themselves managing major accounts. This can happen immediately if they land unusually large customers, or it can happen gradually over time as small customers grow into big ones.

Regardless of how you acquire a big customer, it deserves very special treatment. Just like a precious and delicate flower that has been put into your care, you must nurture it so it prospers. If it gets enough of the right attention, it can be yours forever. But if it doesn't, it will shrivel up and become nothing more than a hole in the ground. Or even worse, a hole in your wallet. So if you want big customers to be yours forever, you have to maintain a healthy relationship.

In many ways, maintaining a healthy business relationship is no different than maintaining a healthy personal relationship. You must first understand what the other person needs and then provide it in a way that also satisfies your own. If both parties' needs are fulfilled in a mutually beneficial way, then the relationship will grow. If not, one party will feel neglected or exploited, and the relationship will begin to disintegrate.

Smart companies therefore put procedures in place to ensure that the needs of their important customers are being met. Examples of such procedures would be strategic account plans or account management activities in various forms. They essentially define how companies want their salespeople to navigate these crucial relationships, and they do so by outlining the steps required to identify and satisfy each other's needs.

If nothing else, account management procedures are useful for encouraging regular, meaningful communication between sellers and their important customers. They typically prescribe a cadence where salespeople should meet with their customers' decision-makers to reaffirm their understanding of the customers' strategic goals. This allows the sellers to remain aligned with their major accounts and to continually add value.

But when regular, meaningful communications don't take place between sellers and their important customers, the two begin to drift apart. Then it's only a matter of time before a dumbstruck salesperson looks up to discover that their formerly loyal customer is now with a competitor. In fact, that unfaithful customer has probably been cheating behind the seller's back for quite a while. And most disturbingly, the jilted seller never saw it coming.

> *When regular, meaningful communications don't take place between sellers and their important customers, the two begin to drift apart*

THE WORST PRACTICE

I was working with a manufacturer to address several problem areas the executive team had identified within its sales force. Of particular concern was the fact that their field salespeople's revenues were highly concentrated in a small number of large accounts. In fact, a recent analysis had shown that more than 70% of the company's sales were coming from only 10% of its customers. They were nervous that some of these top customers might defect to their competitors, which would severely damage the company's growth.

In response to this fear, our team proposed that they implement an account planning process for those customers that comprised the top 10%. At the time, there were no formal sales processes in place, and each salesperson managed accounts with varying degrees of thoroughness and consistency. Putting a little structure in place to bolster these relationships could only have a positive effect.

In short order, we developed a basic account plan for the salespeople to use that would facilitate deliberate interactions with these top customers. In essence, the plan was for the sellers to approach their biggest customers and ask them these three questions:

1. How satisfied are you with the products that we are providing you?
2. What are your strategic goals for next two years?
3. How can we help you achieve those goals?

In our minds, this was about as straightforward as we could make an account management process. Formal sales processes are notoriously bewildering, so we were quite pleased with its simplicity and expected very little pushback from the sales force. What a naïve assumption that turned out to be.

One of the first salespeople we engaged in this process immediately informed us that he would not be participating in the initiative. In fact, he was quite disturbed at the *thought* of posing these three questions to his customers. Ironically, of the top 10% of the customers that we were targeting with the effort, only one of the accounts was assigned to him. In other words, we were asking him to ask these three questions to one executive in one of his accounts. Three questions, one person, one company. How hard could this be?

Me: I have to admit I'm having a hard time understanding your objection to the account-planning process. It doesn't seem like it will be that much of a burden for you.

Reluctant Salesperson: It's not that it will be a burden for me. It will be *embarrassing* for me.

Me: What do you mean? How could this embarrass you?

Salesperson: Look, I've known the president of this company for 15 years. Our kids go to school together. I've talked to this guy at least twice a week for a decade. If I go to this guy and ask him these questions, he's going to think I'm out of my mind.

Me: Why?

Salesperson: I already told you, I talk to this guy all the time. He's my best customer. He's a friend. I know what he wants, and I know what he's trying to accomplish. That's why he gives us almost all of his business—he loves us. I'd feel stupid asking him those questions, like I've never even met the guy.

Me: I understand what you're saying, but just humor us. This new process is a big deal for your company, and the leadership team is expecting everyone to participate. If you give it a little thought, I bet you can come up with a way to make the conversation less awkward than you think it's going to be.

Salesperson: Okay, then. I understand that this is a company-wide thing and everyone has to do it. Let me think about how to spin it, and I'll have a conversation with him next week.

Of course, all of the salespeople had a similar reaction, because these were their biggest customers. They *did* spend a lot of time with them, and they did talk to them all the time. However, regular communication isn't the same as meaningful communication. Saying hello and patting someone on the back twice a week doesn't yield a lot of strategic insights. These facts were perfectly reflected in the next conversation I had with the first reluctant salesperson.

> *Me*: So how did it go with your customer last week? Were you able to get your three questions answered without it being too awkward?

> *Salesperson*: Boy, I sure did. I can't tell you how happy I am that you made me do that.

> *Me* (genuinely surprised by his enthusiasm): Really?

> *Salesperson*: Yeah, I learned a lot. Before I walked into that guy's office last week, I would have sworn that we had 90% of his business. It turns out that we have only about 40%. A competitor of ours has the other 60%.

> *Me*: Wow. That's surprising, given the volume of products he buys just from you.

> *Salesperson*: I know. And when I asked him why he was buying so much product from our competitor, he said it was because the competitor is willing to ship products di-

rectly to *his* customers, which eliminates his cost of warehousing and delivering the products.

Me: Huh.

Salesperson: Exactly. And it's totally ridiculous that we're losing business to a competitor for that reason, because we can do exactly the same thing. In fact, if he would buy that volume of products from us and we could ship directly to his customers, I could undercut the competitor's prices and *still* make more profit than we're making right now. That conversation has totally changed my relationship with him ... for the better. I can't believe what I didn't know.

Me: Well, that sounds like a breakthrough.

Salesperson: No doubt. I can probably boost my revenue from this guy by 50% or more next year with very little effort. I really can't express how shocking this exercise was. I guess sometimes you don't know someone as well as you think you do.

How true it is. Sometimes frequent, superficial conversations masquerade as intimacy, and once-good assumptions become deadly misunderstandings. This is the reason that sales processes are useful, and it's why formal account planning is an absolute must for your high-value customers. Even experienced, talented salespeople become comfortable and inattentive in long-term relationships, and your customers eventually begin to wander. Don't lose a big one because you're afraid to ask a few embarrassing questions.

THE GOOD IDEAS

GOOD IDEA 1: INSTITUTIONALIZE INTIMACY WITH YOUR MOST VALUABLE CUSTOMERS

If a minority of your customers constitute the majority of your business, you must stay engaged with them at a very deep level. Put formal procedures in place to learn what they're thinking and what they need at all times. Familiarity leads to complacency, and complacency leads to neglect. Have frequent, meaningful conversations, or else risk losing your customers' allegiance to their new best friend: your competitor.

GOOD IDEA 2: ASSUME YOUR COMPETITORS ARE ALWAYS LURKING

If you have customers that buy from you on an ongoing basis, it's tempting to believe that they will be loyal forever. And the longer your relationships last, the more loyalty you might expect. However, your competitors are smart enough to find your customers, and your customers are smart enough to entertain a better deal. If a better offer comes along, they just might take it. Then you'll be the one lurking around, searching for a way back in.

CHAPTER TEN

KILL THE MONSTER WHILE IT'S SMALL

THE CONTEXT

For salespeople, encountering objections is a part of life. As prospects proceed through their buying process, it's inevitable that they will encounter information that will give them pause. They will stop to question whether they should proceed with the purchase or abort the mission. In other words, they will object. Sometimes the objections are totally legitimate, and sometimes they're completely absurd, but salespeople have to resolve them nonetheless. Otherwise, a promising sale will come to a screeching halt.

'Objection handling' is therefore a topic that is commonly found in sales training programs. The more prepared salespeople are to handle objections, the more comfortably and confidently they can discharge them. This training will often describe the most frequent objections that sellers can expect to encounter and then provide them with thoughtful responses to appease the buyers' concerns. For instance:

Common Objection: *Your price is way higher than your competitor's.*

Thoughtful Response: *Yes, I've heard that from other customers as well, but once they saw the richness of our features, they totally understood how our product is superior to the competitor's and why the marginally higher cost is justified by a greater return on investment.*

Objection-handling skills are very important and useful, but some of the supposed wisdom that gets dispensed on the topic is laughable. One of my favorites is: 'It is a *great* sign when customers raise objections, because it shows that they're interested.' Umm ... maybe. I think when customers raise objections, it shows that they don't like something about the salesperson or the product. A much better sign is when they don't object at all. That means that the salesperson and the product are both doing their jobs.

Another classic gem is: 'The best way to handle an objection is just to ignore it, because the buyer will either forget they raised it, or they'll answer the objection themselves in their mind.' Umm ... no. If your buyer raises an objection and you don't address it, it's not going away—it's just going unresolved. It will resurface later in the sales cycle and sink your chances of winning the deal, while you excitedly update your sales forecast to reflect the smooth sales call

> *Objection-handling skills are very important and useful, but some of the supposed wisdom that gets dispensed on the topic is laughable*

you just conducted. I sometimes try to ignore the weeds that grow in my lawn, but they never seem to go away. Instead, they tend to grow bigger despite my proactive neglect.

And this leads me to my all-time favorite insane approach to 'handling' objections. In fact, it is the exact opposite of the 'ignore it' strategy. This one states: 'Address all possible objections *before* your customer has the chance to raise them.' Then your customer's mind will be carefree, and those pesky objections won't interfere with the rest of your sale. Yeah, right.

THE WORST PRACTICE

Management consultants are frequently asked to 'shadow' salespeople in the field. In other words, you follow the sellers around and observe them in their natural environment, hoping to gain some insight into their skills or behaviors. It was during one of these shadowing exercises that I first encountered the dubious strategy of frontloading a sales call with all potential objections.

I was riding around with a well-regarded salesperson for a software company. On this particular day, he had an important meeting with a prospect that he'd been pursuing for several months. The meeting was with a team of mid-level managers who had been chosen to evaluate solution providers and narrow the field to two options for their executive team to then interview. Therefore, this was a critical point in the sales cycle—if the salesperson messed up this meeting, he would be knocked out of contention.

The seller and I were discussing his plan for the meeting over breakfast that morning:

Me: So, do you mind sharing with me your agenda for today's big sales call?

Seller: Sure. I'll open the meeting with introductions, since I haven't met a few of the people who will be in the room. I'll introduce myself and then ask them to introduce themselves, telling me what they'd like to accomplish during our time together.

Me: Sounds good.

Seller: Then I'll take five or ten minutes to address several objections that they'll have.

Me: What objections? You will have done only the introductions at this point in the meeting. What kind of objections could they possibly raise to introductions?

Seller: No, no, no. Of course they won't have raised any objections at that point, but I always like to go ahead and address the objections that I know they're going to have.

Me: So, you're going to raise their objections *for them*?

Seller: Sure. People always have the same objections, so I just handle them up front. That way we can get them out of the way, and they don't sit there with the objections festering in their minds. You know, kill the monster while it's small. That way it doesn't grow into something you can't defeat.

Me [willing to learn something new]: Okay. Let's see how it goes.

True to his plan, the salesperson opened the meeting with a round of introductions and wrote the attendees' goals for the meeting on a flip chart. He then launched his preemptive strike.

Seller: So I thought I would begin by addressing some of the concerns that you probably have regarding our company and our products.

The buyers cocked their heads slightly to the side as they looked at the salesperson standing in front of them. Clearly this was not the agenda item that they were expecting to hear immediately after the introductions.

Seller: Many people are concerned about the small size of our company relative to our much larger competitors. In fact, this will be an advantage to you if we earn your business, because we will assign a senior team to you that will be much more capable, attentive, and responsive than our competitors can provide you.

I noted a few nods around the table. Perhaps this was actually a good strategy?

Seller: You might also find that the pricing I'm going to show you toward the end of the meeting will be higher than you expect. You should know that we offer a superior product that commands a premium in the marketplace. This too should be comforting to you, because you will be purchasing the absolute best-in-class solution.

I'm pretty sure I observed shock on the face of at least one attendee. They surely didn't see that one coming so early in the conversation.

Seller: And a few customers have told me that they found stories online questioning the security of our technology. I can assure you that our technology is as secure as any of our competition's. In fact, I'd be happy to put you in touch with several of our current customers who have extensively tested our product and will attest to its bullet-proof security protocols.

At least two of the attendees started taking notes after this revelation. I assume they were making reminders to do some online research on the product's security flaws. Apparently this was a hot news flash to them.

So it went for another five minutes. The salesperson must have 'handled' at least a half dozen objections that the buyers may or may not have had before he raised them. He told me afterward that he was happy to have killed all those monsters while they were still small, though I suspect they were small because he'd given birth to them right there in that room.

His stated strategy was to clear the buyers' minds of all their latent objections so they could pay closer attention to his message. To the contrary, he appeared to have burdened them with a collection of new concerns to hold in reserve for later consideration. That, coupled with their general surprise at his unprovoked defensive stand, set a strange tone for the entire discussion. They seemed to be judging him for the remainder of the meeting, trying to decide if he was the most honest salesperson they had ever met, or just the stupidest. Either way, no sale was made.

I suggested to him that future monster slayings might be better placed at the end of the sales call, rather than the beginning. He disagreed. I can't help but wonder how many of his prospects have stared at him in similar puzzlement throughout his career. Regardless, I've never seen anyone else open a sales call by turning a weapon on himself—inflicting potentially fatal wounds to his sale, not to tiny monsters.

THE GOOD IDEAS

GOOD IDEA 1: DON'T ASSUME YOU KNOW WHAT BUYERS ARE THINKING

Part of the sales challenge is to uncover buyers' needs, so you can then try to satisfy them. As a corollary, you also have to uncover their objections, so you can try to dispel them. But you can't pretend to know what your prospects are thinking— you have to ask them questions to uncover the truth. Making assumptions about their state of mind or their state of affairs is high-risk behavior. Behavior that will cost you sales.

GOOD IDEA 2: NEVER RAISE OBJECTIONS ON BEHALF OF BUYERS

During the course of a sale, there will be plenty of forces campaigning against you—ferocious competitors, skeptical buyers, and market detractors, just to name a few. Don't join their team. There's nothing to be gained by printing your own bad press. Raising objections on behalf of your prospects won't make you appear more proactive or credible. It will just make you appear more objectionable.

CHAPTER ELEVEN

THE CUSTOMER JUST DOESN'T GET IT

THE CONTEXT

Innovation is both the best friend and the worst enemy of the sales force. On one hand, product innovation creates differentiation in the marketplace, which is a great thing for the sellers of the product. Until the competition finds a way to either replicate the innovation or minimize its perceived value to buyers, salespeople have in their bag a uniquely differentiated product that *should* be easier to sell and more resistant to pricing pressure.

However, innovation also places a burden on the salespeople to educate their customers on the merits of the new product or service. And the more innovative the product, the greater that burden can be. Products that are well-known have apparent value propositions, established purchasing processes, and low risks of failure. New products suffer the exact opposites—questionable value, elusive buyers, and high risks.

But the greatest risk during a new product launch comes from the sales force. The company will have invested greatly in the product's development, and expectations will be high. The innovative product will be launched with great fanfare and rosy forecasts, and it's up to the sales force to make the marketing department's dream a marketplace reality. All eyes will be on the salespeople.

Therefore, it takes a highly skilled sales force to launch a new or substantially transformed product. New product launches fail with alarming frequency, and the companies' sales forces are surely to blame for many of those disasters. Often the failures can be attributed to poor product training or otherwise avoidable negligence by management, but sometimes it's just poor skill on the part of the sellers. Particularly, it is the inability of the salesperson to connect the product's innovation to a buyer's needs.

The most common breakdown is a seller's compulsion to simply spew product features and functions all over the unsuspecting buyer—particularly if the product is highly technical in nature. "This product has 50 times the giga-baubles as the previous model with 400% more mega-jiggies and one half as many micro-things." The classic show-up-and-throw-up salesperson will never be more comfortable than during a high-tech product launch. It is a feature-and-function nirvana.

But the biggest challenge to the salesperson in selling an innovative product is to create a vision of the future. The good news is that buyers typically want to see it. They are interested in innovation, and they genuinely want to understand how a new product can help them do things better. They are receptive and attentive to the salesperson's pitch—they just need some help catching it.

The most important skill in such a situation is the ability of the seller to climb inside the head of the buyer. As the buyer stands there looking at the seller with raised eyebrows processing the new information, the seller needs to take the buyer slowly and methodically down a path from the buyer's current understanding of the world to a post-innovation understanding of it. Rather than hastily describing the future state, the seller has to drop breadcrumbs every few feet and carefully lead the buyer to the promised land.

> *The classic show-up-and-throw-up sales-person will never be more comfortable than during a high-tech product launch*

In essence, the seller has to pull the buyer into the future rather than push. The buyer shouldn't be expected to intuitively grasp the magnitude of the innovation; the seller has to reveal it in incremental doses that keep the buyer's feet planted in the present while drawing the buyer's gaze toward the future. When the buyer can't see the path from here to there, 'there' looks too distant and too unfamiliar. The leap is too far. Buyers need to take baby steps to travel a great distance, but sellers tend to sell in very long strides. Consequently, the buyer's journey into the future is often abandoned along the way.

THE WORST PRACTICE

I once worked with a startup company that sold a revolutionary technology that would make television advertising 'interactive' for viewers. Much like we click on Internet advertising when we see something that appeals to us, this technology would enable viewers to click on the television screen when they see an actor wearing a sweater they like or driving a car that interests them. It promised to create an entirely new industry of in-program advertising and click-through product placement.

More specifically, this company sold consulting services to develop the interactive content that would appear on the television screen. If you were an advertiser of sweaters or cars, you would hire this company to turn your regular television advertising into interactive advertising by superimposing the click-through technology onto your commercials. The company also integrated that advertising with a virtual shopping cart and other applications to enable the purchase transaction.

On the surface, this was a very cool technology that could dramatically expand the market for e-commerce. However, it was a new technology that required advertisers who were just grappling with the Internet to stretch their thinking even farther onto the television screen. In other words, it was not going to be a simple sale.

I was riding with one of the company's salespeople on a day when she was making sales calls on several global advertising companies. My purpose was only to observe the customer interactions—I was to play no role in the sales calls. Therefore, I merely sat back and watched three interactions that pretty much went like this:

> *Seller*: I'm sure you're going to be blown away by this new technology, and you'll quickly see how it will enable you to grow your sales by exploiting a totally new marketplace.

[The seller shows a five-minute video of the technology applied to actual television shows where the advertiser could put a product placement.]

Seller: You can see how viewers would find this to be a compelling experience and jump at the opportunity to buy your products from within the show.

Buyer: What technology platform are you using to enable the interaction?

Seller: We've developed a proprietary platform of <technical gibberish that the buyer doesn't understand>. We then connect to a backend application that <more technical gibberish>. And this enables the viewers to connect with our transactional database using <yet more gibberish>.

Buyer (trying to ground the new technology in something familiar): So how is this similar to the Internet advertising that I'm currently doing online?

Seller: This is a *totally* different experience for the viewer. The two are light years apart in their technical sophistication.

Buyer: But it's basically just click-through advertising on a television screen instead of a computer screen, right?

Seller: I wouldn't recommend that you think of it like that. Remember the <previous gibberish> that I mentioned? This <gibberish> is built on <other gibberish>

that makes traditional Internet advertising look like Stone-Age technology.

Buyer: But functionally, it still just seems like click-through advertising. But on a television.

Seller: No, you can't think of it that way. That's completely ignoring our extreme technical advances that made this possible. <Gibberish, gibberish, gibberish.>

This futile exercise continued for another 15 minutes, until the meeting finally came to an end. At which time, the buyer concluded that he would "need time to think about it." We then exchanged smiles and handshakes, and we were escorted out of the building. All three sales calls that day followed this script almost identically.

Also identical were the salesperson's post-meeting reactions. After each failed sales call, the seller would stop just outside of the office building, put her hands on her hips, stare at me blankly, and say "Man, that person just didn't get it." Then she would stare at the ground, shake her head, and look at me once more to repeat, "They just don't get it." She'd shrug her shoulders, and then off we'd go to our next doomed meeting.

And to some extent, the salesperson was right. The buyer did not 'get it.' But what the *seller* didn't get is that it's not the prospect's responsibility to get it. Much to the contrary, it's the seller's responsibility to give it. The burden should not be on the buyer to connect all the dots that reveal a beautiful image of the future—it is the seller's responsibility to paint that picture for him. That's why companies hire salespeople … to sell.

Uttering the phrase "The customer doesn't get it" has come to represent in my mind the highest form of self-incrimination for a bad salesperson. If a seller can conduct an entire meeting with a receptive buyer and not effectively connect the buyer's needs to her product's capabilities, then that salesperson has failed at her job. And blaming the *buyer* for a wasted sales call is completely laughable. Make no mistake—a failed sales call is never the fault of the buyer. It's *always* the fault of the seller. Period. To think otherwise is insane.

THE GOOD IDEAS

GOOD IDEA 1: THE SELLER MUST DO THE HEAVY LIFTING IN A SALES CALL

There may be two people involved in a typical sales call, but the burden of a productive meeting is not split between them. The burden lies fully with the seller to facilitate value creation for the buyer. Blaming the buyer for a failed sales call is the worst type of delusion, because it vindicates the person responsible for the failure and blames the person who was the unwitting victim of sales malpractice. When you leave a failed sales call, don't bemoan the buyer's ignorance. Find the nearest mirror and ask it what really went wrong.

GOOD IDEA 2: SELLING INNOVATION REQUIRES AN ADVANCED SKILL SET

As much as we deride the show-up-and-throw-up salesperson as a relic of the past, the truth is that many salespeople still can (and do) succeed by playing the role of a feature-and-function robot. But when it's time to sell a disruptive technology or innovation, those sales reps will fail miserably. The ability to pull buyers delicately down the path from a world they know to a world they *could* know is beyond many sellers. It requires a level of restraint and awareness that is counter to the way many sellers view themselves. If you're launching a truly innovative product, think carefully about which of your salespeople are up to the task and which ones will merely leave your prospects flummoxed.

CHAPTER TWELVE

IT'S ALL OR NOTHING, MR. BUYER

THE CONTEXT

In our haste to sell stuff, it's all too easy to forget about our buyers. Not to forget that they exist, of course—we fully understand that we're selling to entities known as buyers. Rather, we fail to appreciate the fact that *they* are the ones with the real problems. The sales force has a goal to continually feed its company's hunger for revenue, but that's not really a problem. Sales only encounters a problem when it fails to reach its goal. Truth is, there's nothing inherently problematic about being in sales.

But all buyers have problems that they are trying to resolve. Whether it's a company trying to fix operational failures or an individual trying to remove some personal discomfort, buyers go into the marketplace only after they've identified that they have an issue that needs to be resolved. And somewhere along their journey to resolve that issue, they will encounter a seller who offers to help.

It's my observation that most buyers are highly motivated to solve their problems, and most are fairly forthright with salespeople. Sure, buyers will be coy when discussing your competitors, and they can color the truth when it's time to negotiate. But most buyers are generally sincere, because they are the ones with the most to lose. When sellers lose a sale, they have dozens more in their sales pipeline to go pursue. But if buyers fail to find a solution, then they've visibly wasted their time and money. And worse yet, they still have the problems.

Consequently, I'm surprised by the degree to which sellers view their buyers as adversaries. It's as though salespeople are inherently suspicious of buyers, who are perceived to have the upper hand and are willing to use it. Of course, buyers can be equally suspicious of sellers, who are perceived to be self-interested and motivated only to make a sale. The buyer-seller dynamic can be so contentious and fraught with distrust, it's a wonder that any transactions ever get consummated.

Regardless of the buyers' perceptions of us sellers, we should give them the benefit of the doubt. Again, they have more to lose than we do if the deal goes badly, because they have to live with the consequences longer and at a more personal level. Perhaps we should take their statements at face value by default. Otherwise, we engage in a dance of

> *The buyer-seller dynamic can be so contentious and fraught with distrust, it's a wonder that any transactions ever get consummated*

deception that's both frustrating and unproductive for us both.

THE WORST PRACTICE

I once partnered with another management consultant to pursue a project that required a large, diverse team. The other consultant was a very experienced professional with many more hard-earned gray hairs than I had at the time. Therefore, it was both logical and expected that he was the lead dog, and my pack and I were to follow him wherever he chose to take us.

To be candid, this comforted me somewhat. The project we were pursuing was quite complex, and the prospect was a very large, highly visible financial services firm. It calmed me to know that the more senior consultant had sold and managed many projects like this in his past, and this would be a rare opportunity to observe a master at work. If only it had happened that way.

For several years, the company had been experiencing extremely high turnover in its customer base, losing two-thirds of its clients when their bank accounts came up for renewal. That amounted to millions of dollars they were hemorrhaging every single month. The project we designed to stop the bleeding was quite comprehensive. We would investigate every possible root cause for why its customers were defecting, and then we'd attack the issues from every possible angle. There was little doubt in our minds or the minds of our prospects that the project would yield the desired results.

As we began to draft our final proposal for the company's executive team, we received a call from the head of sales. He said, "It would be great if you could tell me the total cost of this project, even if it's just an estimate. I'd like to start socializing the investment behind the scenes to make sure we have enough budget allocated to do this work in the current fiscal year."

At this point we had a fairly specific estimate for the cost of the project we were going to propose: $1.2 million. Yet our lead dog refused to share that number with the head of sales. "We haven't yet shown them all of the value they're going to get from this project," he said to me. "Until they acknowledge how valuable our help will be, we can't tell them the cost. It would just lead to a premature negotiation of our price." And so we didn't tell them.

The sales leader asked us at least twice more (that I knew of) to give him an estimated cost for the project. He continued to claim that he realized it was going to be a big investment, and he wanted to make certain he had the budget approved before presenting it to the larger committee. But we didn't. Lead Dog was confident we should not "show our hand," as though we were playing some high-stakes poker game. In his mind, the executive was an adversary to be combatted in our sales process.

Eventually the big reveal took place, as we laid out our plan for the executive team and disclosed to all the price tag of $1.2 million. The buyers were impressively stoic as the surely shocking number was discussed. Afterward, they predictably informed us they would need to discuss it among themselves before giving us the final go-ahead to begin work the following week.

I should note that all of this transpired at a point in my career where every dollar mattered. My colleagues and I had started our small consulting firm only one year earlier, and this project would provide us with desperately needed cash flow. My relief after this meeting was immense. It looked as if we would continue to make our monthly payroll.

Then a week passed without any contact from the presumptive client. Then two weeks, then three. Lead Dog characterized the silence as "very strange." I found it nothing short of terrifying.

Eventually, the head of sales requested a group phone call with our team. He told us that the executive committee had authorized $350,000 for the first phase of the project, and they would release the remainder of the project's funds once the effort had "demonstrated results." The head of sales was himself very concerned about this, because he realized that the first phase of the project was merely data collection and analysis. As our project plan was currently defined, there would literally be no results whatsoever for the first $350,000. He was basically asking us to redefine our project.

"Is there any way you can re-work your project plan so that we realize some tangible benefits after this first $350,000? It's not that we don't have the entire $1.2 million to spend, but that number caught some of the committee members off guard. We just need to put some points on the board so the committee is confident you will deliver as you promise."

"No," responded Lead Dog. "We designed the project just exactly as it needs to be done. We can conduct the data collection and analysis for $350,000, but we won't get to the point of implementing any actual change until later in the project."

The head of sales (the person with the *real* problem) was nearly pleading as he asked, "Yes, I understand that. But is there any way you could maybe alter your project plan a little to implement some of the most obvious changes we've already identified? That way we can make some progress with the funds we have now and then build some momentum for the rest of the effort."

Lead Dog was unrelenting. "No. This the way we know the project should be done, and this is the way we have to do it. Altering the plan would simply waste your time and money. This is the way we have to do it, if you want the results we've discussed."

As the phone call concluded, I immediately called Lead Dog in an effort to soften his rigid stance on the project. "I think what they're asking for is pretty reasonable," I said. He replied calmly, "They'll find the budget for the whole project. There's too much money to be lost if they don't fund it."

"Well, you have to appreciate their position," I implored (trying not to betray my anxiety). "What happens if this is not a negotiation tactic, and they actually decide to kill the project?" His response was exceedingly blunt: "Then I guess they'll kill it."

And that they did. The project died an immediate death, never to be resurrected. There was no first phase. No second phase. No $350,000. No $1.2 million. Nothing but the continued hemorrhaging of customers by our prospect. At least until they found another more flexible consultant to replace us, which I assume they did. Their problem didn't disappear—only we did.

As you might expect, many post-mortem conversations took place with Lead Dog. In the end, I think our mistake was not taking the head of sales at his word. Lead Dog believed that the executive was starting to negotiate with us when he first requested a budget estimate, though he was probably just doing exactly what he was purporting to do. He wanted to help us help him. And Lead Dog surely believed that the executive team would ultimately order the entire project, despite the fact that they were asking for a bite-sized portion. Wrong again.

They genuinely wanted to work with us, but we weren't responsive to their repeated requests to make it easy for them to buy. We were focused on the selling task and viewed them as adversaries. Instead, if we had taken them at their word and just played nice, everyone would have had a better fiscal year. Even Lead Dog.

THE GOOD IDEAS

GOOD IDEA 1: THE BUYER IS OFTEN MORE MOTIVATED THAN THE SELLER

Buyers are the ones with the actual problems, and they want those problems resolved. By the time they enter into a buying process, they're typically committed to acquiring a solution. They might not be committed to buying it from *you*, but they want to buy it from someone. Take what they say at face value, unless you have a reason to believe they're lying. They have more to lose than you do if the sale goes wrong.

GOOD IDEA 2: IT'S BETTER TO MEET YOUR BUYER'S DEMANDS THAN TO DEMAND THEY MEETS YOURS

There is give-and-take between the buyer and seller in almost every complex sale. But remember this truth: The seller exists to solve the buyer's problem, not vice versa. If the buyer continues to pull you in their direction, then it's often best to yield your position. Pull too hard and the buyer will give up. You'll be left with nothing, and the buyer will simply find someone to replace you. Your competitor's salespeople are remarkably easy to locate.

PART III
SALES
MANAGEMENT
INSANITY

CHAPTER THIRTEEN

CRM OR BUST

THE CONTEXT

When Customer Relationship Management (CRM) arrived in the late 1990s, it was guaranteed to be a game changer. Most companies had installed vast Enterprise Resource Planning (ERP) tools to run their back offices, and there was a strong desire to create equally efficient operations in their customer-facing organizations. CRM was being sold as a utopian dream for senior sales leaders—visibility into and control over the revenue-generating machine.

This was a particularly easy sell for CRM vendors, since sales was considered by many top executives to be a mysterious black box. Into it went tons of resources, and out of it came some revenue. What happened inside the box was less transparent than in any other business function. Unlike finance or operations, sales did not typically have neatly defined processes, nor insightful performance metrics, nor (most importantly) nerve-calming management reports.

Into this void of sales discipline, CRM offered a better tomorrow. Sales would finally become integrated with marketing. Leads would be tracked. Sales would have processes. Efficiencies would be realized. Customers would be nurtured. With CRM in place, executives would finally be able to manage the sales force just like ERP allowed them to manage their operations.

What can't be appreciated so many years later is how sincerely and universally senior executives viewed CRM as a strategic weapon. Now, CRM is a well-entrenched component of the corporate infrastructure—just like telephones, e-mail, and the Internet. But back in time, executives were scrambling to install CRM at any cost out of fear that their competitors would beat them to the punch. Literally, it was an information-technology gold rush of historic proportion. Money was no object, nor was sales management's sanity in handling the chaos. For many organizations, it was CRM or bust.

> *What can't be appreciated so many years later is how sincerely and universally senior executives viewed CRM as a strategic weapon*

THE WORST PRACTICE

I was managing a team of process consultants for a mid-sized consulting firm. The phone call came one day from a major technology company that needed some process design work done to accompany new CRM software it was implementing. This didn't seem so odd, except that the implementation was already underway. Why were they just now asking for process documentation if they had already begun to build the system? And what were they automating? Air? Here is what I learned:

A year or two before, the company had elected to implement the 'best of breed' CRM tool to automate its sales force's key activities. Basically, this was the biggest and most robust of all the CRM applications on the market at the time. (Note: If you ever hear that a new system has been chosen because it has 'robust' capabilities, you're probably starting down a dark, scary path).

Simultaneously, the company had engaged one of the biggest consulting firms in the world to handle the customization and deployment of the new CRM software. So far, so good. The company had in fact chosen a very safe road to the promised land by purchasing the state-of-the-art CRM application and hiring a marquee systems integrator to bring it to life.

Things first started to go wrong during the contract negotiations with the big consulting firm. The systems integrator had quoted a preliminary figure of $20 million to design and implement the new CRM tool. The company's chief information officer, fancying himself a master negotiator, felt that it was his sole job to reduce this nose-bleed figure, and he responded with a classic negotiating strategy. He simply countered that the price was outrageous.

This old-school, price-is-outrageous negotiating strategy can work okay when you're purchasing a clearly defined product—like a car, for instance. You can see what you are purchasing, and the price is eventually the only variable left on the table. You negotiate back and forth, and one party's gain is the other party's loss. A low final price is a victory for the buyer, since they get the same car regardless of the price.

However, consulting services are not clearly defined products, and there are at least two variables in play until the very end—the price for the work and the *scope* of the work. Savvy consultants respond to the price-is-too-high bargaining tactic by offering to lower the price along with the scope of work to be performed. Basically, the profit margin for the consultant stays the same while the amount of work decreases. In truth, this is a totally legitimate solution for both the client and the consultant, as long as the client understands what's being eliminated from the scope of work. And, of course, as long as what's being eliminated is not critical to the success of the effort.

The CIO in this case battered the systems integrator down to $12 million by eliminating all of the business consulting around the technology: that is, the process definition, the business logic, the work flow, etc. Basically, this was all the stuff that the CRM tool was meant to automate. Unfortunately, the CIO's negotiating stance was based on a highly erroneous assumption—that all of this 'business' stuff either already existed inside the company or else it could be quickly developed by the company's own employees. Therefore, the only task of the consultant would be to build the CRM application around all the business stuff that the company would provide.

Thus began the hiring of dozens of additional consultants like me, as sales, marketing, and operations were now being asked by the systems integrator for all the business content to be automated—content which, of course, didn't exist. Therefore, the consulting budget was effectively spread throughout the organization and quickly began to speed past the original $20-million estimate to fully develop the CRM capability.

To make matters worse, the functionality of the system to be implemented began to expand. What began as a fairly contained scope of automating order entry and other basic tasks became an ever-expanding wish list of CRM features. If they were going to automate order entry, then they might as well automate the pricing process too. Then it was revealed by the expert CRM sales team that the system could also configure complex product bundles for the salespeople—so better do that, too. And the system could also integrate with the existing ERP tool to make all kinds of things work more smoothly. Add that to the list.

The growing scope of CRM functionality and the consequent demands on the business to define the underlying processes spiraled out of control in a way that can only be defined as insane. My team and I were only one of many consulting firms there, and we worked on this project for over two years. You can see where this is going.

In the end, I was told that the company spent—get ready—*$90 million* on this CRM tool. $15 million went to the CRM vendor for software licenses and another $75 million went to technology and business consultants. $90 million! Just a *bit* more than the outlandish $20 million which so offended the CIO. Yet this is not even the most amazing fact of this story.

Even more staggering than the amount that they 'invested' in this CRM tool is the remarkable fact that *no salesperson ever used it*. The system was never successfully deployed. Several years, three CIOs, and $90 million later, the company gave up on the system as the economy slowed and the company's finances went south. In fact, you won't be surprised to learn that this company no longer exists. Nor the CRM vendor, actually. Only the consultants.

THE GOOD IDEAS

GOOD IDEA 1: TECHNOLOGY IS JUST AN ENABLER OF BUSINESS PROCESSES

Technology is too often sold as the silver bullet cure-all for any business issue. In reality, technology is just an enabler. It won't solve any problems on its own—it will just help you do the wrong things faster. Attempting to automate chaos is one classic foible, as is assuming that a new system will provide you with embedded Best Practices. Take the time to define how you want your business to work *before* you set about automating it. Otherwise, a technology implementation could become a very expensive and disruptive way to ruin your career.

GOOD IDEA 2: WHEN IMPLEMENTING TECHNOLOGY, THINK SMALL

'Big bang' system implementations are always tinged with insanity. My counsel to clients is always the same: Implement the smallest piece of technology that you can possibly imagine, and then build the functionality in bite-sized pieces. If you're replacing your current CRM tool, start by replicating the existing tool's functionality. If you're implementing a tool for the first time, think very carefully about which critical activities you really need to automate. Then add the bells and whistles. Otherwise, the sound you hear won't be all the bells and whistles working in the background, it will be sound of an oncoming train.

CHAPTER FOURTEEN

WE'D BE BETTER OFF WITHOUT ALL THESE SELLERS

The following vignette is unlike others in this book, be-cause I didn't participate directly in the madness. This is also the only company that I will not discuss anonymously, since it all took place in the public eye. Though this story (and the company) is now a distant memory, it remains a timeless tale of bad executive judgment.

THE CONTEXT

It's not easy to be a consumer products retailer. There are lots of competitors who sell the same products and lure cus-tomers into their stores with low, low prices. Then there's the Internet, where buyers can find even more competitors, end-less information, expert reviews, customer feedback, and even lower low, low prices. Then there are the economics of run-ning a retail business. It's a thin profit margin, volume-driven industry that spends the entire year holding its collective breath to see whether the holiday shopping season will push it into profitability. It really is a tough gig.

And what of the sales force? Well, the 'sales force' for retailers is the staff of associates who roam the floor and are responsible for offering insight and guidance to inquiring buyers. Unfortunately, insight and guidance is rarely forthcoming from these entry-level sales positions, and I can personally think of no environment where the quality of the salespeople varies more wildly than in a retail store.

To wit, I recently experienced the two extremes of the spectrum when purchasing a laser printer. Unable to make any sense of the contradicting information online, I drove to two local stores to inspect their inventory and ask for some advice. In the first store, I had a great shopping experience. The nearest associate approached me, asked a few probing questions about my intended usage of the machine, narrowed the choices for me based on my responses, and then gave me his credible perspective on which units were more dependable. A very valuable interaction. He was a good salesperson.

At the second store, I had a much less valuable shopping experience. Instead of asking me any questions, the associate pulled the little paper tabs off the front of a few printers—the tabs that have bullet points printed on them with the features and functions of the products. He then stood there reading the bullet points aloud to me, as though I hadn't already read them for myself within 30 seconds of enter-

> *I can personally think of no environment where the quality of the salespeople varies more wildly than in a retail store*

ing the store. Here was a useless salesperson. I then returned to the first store and purchased the printer that the good salesperson had recommended.

Two things are noteworthy about my laser printer story. First, I could have purchased the printer cheaper online. Instead, I chose to indulge myself in spite of the incremental cost of a brick-and-mortar establishment so I could see the printers in person. This, along with the immediacy of the acquiring a product, is one of the only advantages of visiting retail store versus purchasing the product online ... A richer buying experience.

Second, the interaction with a salesperson in a retail store can have a profound effect on the buyer's decision-making process. In my case, it was the single factor that funneled my $700 into one store's register instead of their competitor's. And it was the only reason I chose not buy the same printer for $600 online. Even in a big-box retail store, salespeople are very important. Unless, apparently, that store was Circuit City.

THE WORST PRACTICE: ROUND 1

Circuit City's first bout with sales insanity came in 2003. Though it was once the dominant big-box electronics retailer, Circuit City had by then fallen far behind archrival Best Buy, and its earnings were on a slow road to nowhere. To pull itself out of the death spiral, it crafted a novel and potentially potent strategy—focus on its customers.

Circuit City's 2003 Annual Report began: "In fiscal 2003, our focus on the customer continued to serve as the foundation for our effort to improve sales, profits, and returns for Circuit City shareholders." The report went on to declare that "differentiating Circuit City with a high-service shopping experience remains our primary strategy." In fact, "It is the shopping experience that tells our customers 'We're with you.'" Sounds like a decent plan. But how would they accomplish this feat?

To create an impressive service experience that is focused on its customers, it seems kind of obvious that Circuit City would need to rely on its sales associates—its salespeople in the stores who actually interact with customers. These face-to-face interactions are really what define the customer's shopping experience. Management's only task then would be to get the sales associates to focus on their customers. So what did Circuit City do in 2003 to help its salespeople improve their customer focus? Ready yourself for the insanity.

Circuit City started by eliminating all sales commissions. That's right. Circuit City's management removed the only systemic motivation that their sales associates had to even interact with a customer in the store—a commission that was earned by helping the customer make an informed buying decision. No need for that, I guess. An hourly pay rate should be just as motivating as a commission.

For their part, management thought that the new hourly pay structure was brilliant. It would apparently "Unify our Sales Associates into one team, focused solely on customer service." Umm ... maybe. They also predicted that the removal of commissions would "Increase browse time in our stores." Because that's the goal? Shouldn't Circuit City have wanted to encourage its salespeople to try to *close* sales rather than just stand around and watch prospective buyers browse?

To clear up any confusion about the objective of the sales associate's role, management also thought it wise to remove the term "sales" from their titles and rename them "Product Specialist." Not Customer Specialists or even Service Specialists, but *Product* Specialists. Because nothing says "our focus is on the customer" quite like providing the customer with a product specialist.

Management also came up with another clever way to create a "high-service shopping experience" for their customers. They decided to reduce the number of associates by 1,800—approximately three per store. So we now have 1,800 fewer "Product Specialists" with no incentive to sell. To be fair, management did admit that they anticipated a "short-term sales disruption resulting from this change." They got that right.

From Circuit City's 2004 Annual Report:

We were disappointed by the comparable store merchandise sales decline in fiscal 2004. ... Our store Associates worked through major changes in the operating model during fiscal 2004, and we believe that store execution suffered as a result. This weak execution was reflected in an overall reduction in customer satisfaction levels. Higher-than-normal turnover in store-level management contributed to the reduction.

As a result of their "customer-focused" strategy, sales declined, execution suffered, customer satisfaction tanked, and store-level management threw in the towel. What a success. For the record, they did save $130 million by eliminating commissions and reducing headcount—but their revenues declined by $208 million.

Despite these early and strong signals that their strategy might be failing, senior management was unwavering in their confidence as they pronounced, "In fiscal 2005, we will refocus on execution and the consistent delivery of outstanding customer service in all stores." Albert Einstein famously defined insanity as doing the same thing over and over again and expecting different results. Well ...

THE WORST PRACTICE: ROUND 2

Circuit City's second run of sales insanity came in 2007. At this time they were only two years away from totally liquidating their bankrupt company, but they still had some sales management tricks up their sleeves. Their 2007 Annual Report stated that they were "continuing to challenge all aspects of our SG&A expense." It seems that the poor, aimless Product Specialists were still in the crosshairs.

In March 2007, Circuit City issued a press release announcing the following:

The company has completed a wage management initiative that will result in the separation of approximately 3,400 store Associates. The separations, which are occurring today, focused on Associates who were paid well above the market-based salary range for their role. New Associates will be hired for these positions and compensated at the current market range for the job.

In other words, Circuit City fired all of their highest-paid salespeople and replaced them with new hires. It didn't take a seasoned sales consultant to see the insanity in this behavior—at the time a Wall Street analyst commented "It's definitely going to have some cost-savings, but I think the bigger impact could be seen in weaker, poor service. I have a feeling the people they're letting go have probably been there longer, have more experience, more product knowledge." Bingo.

So in pursuit of their customer-focused shopping nirvana, management chose to fire en masse the most knowledgeable employees in the company and replace them with a team of low-paid salespeople who knew no more about their products than what was printed in bullet points on the paper tags in front of the printers. Brilliant indeed.

Reportedly, the talent-swap was "expected to reduce expenses for the electronics retailer by $110 million in fiscal year 2008 and $140 million a year starting in fiscal 2009. Circuit City said sales would be "volatile for the next several months as the company adjusts to the changes."[1] Again proving to be superb prognosticators, sales were *incredibly* volatile over the next 24 months, going from around $12 billion to precisely zero. But hey, they saved much more than their estimated $140 million in fiscal 2009, since they were able to fire *all* their associates. Now *that* is cost savings.

THE GOOD IDEAS

GOOD IDEA 1: THE SALES FORCE IS THE CUSTOMER EXPERIENCE

Companies should never lose sight of one important fact: At the beginning of every customer relationship, the salesperson defines the company in the buyer's eyes. No matter how good a company's products, and no matter how strong its brand, the sales force *is* the customer experience as the relationship begins. Degrade the sales force at your own peril.

---

[1] Ylan Q. Mui, Washington Post, Thursday, March 29, 2007; Page D01

GOOD IDEA 2: GOOD SALESPEOPLE ARE WORTH EVERY PENNY

It seems to me that there are two types of people: Those who think salespeople should never make more money than their managers, and those who think salespeople should make more money than their CEO. I've always considered the latter type to be the saner group of folks. Every company should acknowledge that its fortunes are derived from the people on the front lines. Don't begrudge top salespeople for earning lots of money, congratulate them and say "thank you" for a job well done.

CHAPTER FIFTEEN

OUR SALESPEOPLE SHOULD ENTER THE DATA

THE CONTEXT

Sales productivity is the product of two distinct factors: sales efficiency and sales effectiveness. Though the terms get used interchangeably in casual conversation, efficiency and effectiveness are not the same things. And from a sales management perspective, it's quite useful to understand the difference between the two.

Sales *efficiency* is about the prudent allocation of sales force resources. These resources could be anything from a financial budget to a computer network, but without question the most precious resource in any sales force is time. Time does not discriminate—everyone has the exact same number of hours in the day. No one can manufacture more of it. So achieving sales efficiency is principally the challenge of maximizing the amount of productive time that your sales force has in a day. Eliminate low-value activities, replace them with high-value activities, and your efficiency will be on the rise.

Sales *effectiveness* is not about how you allocate your sales force's resources—it's about how potently you utilize them to accomplish your goals. If you can find a way to squeeze in 20 additional prospecting phone calls for your reps each week, then you've accomplished a feat of efficiency. How skilled your reps are at executing those phone calls is a measure of their effectiveness. A more effective salesperson might produce ten qualified opportunities from those 20 phone calls, while a less effective seller might only create five. More effective salespeople will yield a higher output from the same level of effort, because they just do the task better.

Someone once described the distinction between efficiency and effectiveness in this way: Efficiency is about knocking on as many doors as possible; Effectiveness is about what you do when the doors open. You could call it a dichotomy of 'Will versus Skill' or 'Braun versus Brain,' but the important thing is to understand that there are two different forces at work that influence the productivity of your sales team.

Of course, improving both efficiency and effectiveness is the ultimate objective of good sales management, but you approach these two factors in decidedly different ways. Improving efficiency is often the easier of the two tasks, since it can be accomplished by simply shuffling around tasks on the calendar to make room for more productive effort. Truly, efficiency can be improved today with just a little thought and disci-

> *Efficiency is about knocking on as many doors as possible; Effectiveness is about what you do when the doors open*

pline.

Effectiveness requires a lot more effort to improve, because it involves the development of additional capability on the part of your sales team. Whether that incremental capability comes through training, or coaching, or the implementation of new sales tools, there's almost always a period of learning and adoption that must be endured to reach higher levels of sales effectiveness. Regardless, you always want to be trudging forward on both fronts, and you never, ever, *ever* want to purposefully move backward. For that would be insane.

THE WORST PRACTICE

I was working with the North American division of a global manufacturer. Among other things, we were collaborating with the division's sales operations team to design and deploy a new price-approval process. Because of an economic downturn at the time, the competitive dynamics in the industry necessitated deep discounting off the company's published pricing. Leadership had decided to discount its existing list prices rather than publish new lower pricing, so they wouldn't have to re-raise the prices when the economy turned around.

As we progressed through this project, we encountered the unanticipated barrier of trashy data in the CRM database. I mean really trashy data. We had designed a pricing approval process where the sellers would put a new order into the system, and then the proposed pricing would be routed to a designated 'approver' within the organization based on a combination of criteria like the customer type, product type, requested discount, etc. However, we literally couldn't get past the very first step of the process, because the system was incapable of matching new orders with the existing customers in its database. The process was completely stymied because the data going into the system was just too bad.

As we started digging into the root of the evil, it quickly became apparent that the sellers were the problem. The salespeople in this company were really uncomfortable with computers, and they were especially horrible at data entry. Literally, it was as if everyone's fingers were five times the size of a normal human's digits. It was unbelievable to witness them pecking away at their keyboards. Not only did it take them *forever* to input a new customer order, they were completely mangling the data they were typing into the computer.

As you might expect, we asked a lot of questions about the sales force's lack of computer proficiency. How could this sad state of affairs still exist in the twenty-first century? We heard a litany of observations and excuses from senior leadership that got us nowhere, until I finally had the following conversation with a salesperson in a field office far from the corporate headquarters:

Me: So, we're really having a problem with the new price-approval process, because the quality of the data that the sales team is putting into the system is pretty poor.

Fat-Fingered Seller: I don't doubt that. The system and all of its data entry screens are really hard to use. It takes me maybe ten minutes to put a new order into the system, and maybe fifteen minutes if it's a new customer. It's just brutal. I'm not surprised that there are errors in the data.

Me: Well you've been using that same system for almost five years, and most of the salespeople have been here much longer than that. Why is it still so challenging? Have they changed the user interface or something?

Seller: No, I think the data entry screens are pretty much the same as they've always been, but we never used to enter the customer orders ourselves. That's a new mandate that came from senior management about six months ago.

Me: What do you mean you never used to enter the orders yourself? Who entered them?

Seller: We used to have assistants in each of the sales offices who would enter the orders for us.

Me: Really?

Seller: Yeah, we just told them what the customer wanted, and they put the orders into the system. It probably took them no more than 60 seconds to do it. They really knew the system, since they were in there all the time. I mean, I probably only put in five or six orders per week, while they must have done a hundred.

Me: So why did the assistants go away?

Seller: I don't know. You'd have to ask someone at headquarters.

So I did.

Me (to the VP of Sales): So I understand that the customer orders used to be entered by sales assistants, not the salespeople.

VP of Sales: That's right. But we were under a lot of pressure to cut costs, so we decided to eliminate most of the assistants. They weren't really doing much other than entering new orders and a few other administrative tasks.

Me: Okay. So did you consider just consolidating the order-entry function into a few regional offices, or even to create a small order-entry team here at headquarters?

VP: Yes, we actually did discuss that, but we decided this would be a good time to make the salespeople responsible for the data. We figured they should be accountable since they are the ones who know the customers best. Why should we pay someone else to do their jobs for them?

And there it was. The company had actually put *themselves* in this trashy situation by forcing its salespeople to enter the data. In my mind, this was pretty fat-fingered sales management. By eliminating the relatively low-cost sales assistants (they received about one-third of a salesperson's compensation), management had with one poor decision crushed both their sales force's efficiency *and* its effectiveness. A rare accomplishment indeed.

The sales team's efficiency went down because management made the conscious choice to shift order entry from people who could do it in 60 seconds to people who could barely do it at all. The amount of time the company spent on data entry exploded as a result. Even worse, they assigned a low-value task to a high-value role that had better things to do with two hours per week ... like sell. From a sales efficiency perspective, it was a pretty bad trade.

The sales team's effectiveness also took a hit because the quality of the data being entered plummeted. Where the assistants had become adept at entering the orders, the salespeople were disastrous at doing it. And since they were only entering five or six orders per week, the reps were not riding a very fast learning curve. The data would forever remain trashy, unless the company invested in either improving the system or training its sellers to use a computer.

The decline in effectiveness was ultimately causing trouble in other parts of the company. Most notably, we couldn't implement the price-approval process, because the system couldn't make sense of the mangled data that was being put into it. The company's sagging profit margins would remain low as a consequence. If you add up the lost efficiency in the sales force and the lost profits to the company, those assistants started to look like a pretty good bargain. In fact, the sales force soon started hiring them back into the field offices.

THE GOOD IDEAS

GOOD IDEA 1: PRODUCTIVITY = EFFICIENCY X EFFECTIVENESS

The output of your sales force is driven by both its efficiency and its effectiveness. Efficiency is about prioritizing your activities wisely; Effectiveness is about being good at what you do. Smart sales leaders will pay equal attention to both. Without one, you're wasting time. Without the other, you're wasting effort. Neither of those is a productive way to manage your sales force.

GOOD IDEA 2: SALES SUPPORT IS CHEAP

With the exception of senior management, salespeople are typically the most expensive resources in any company. Administrative support is often the cheapest. If there's any way to offload low-value tasks from your sales team to support staff, then do it today. The increase in efficiency will be almost immediate, and you might even boost your effectiveness too. Don't ask any questions—don't even ask for permission. Just do it. It might be the only Current Best Practice that I will abide.

CHAPTER SIXTEEN

GO CROSS-SELL ... NO, WAIT!

THE CONTEXT

Companies love to purchase other companies. Each year thousands of companies merge with their competitors or acquire companies that offer complementary products to their own. In the case of competitive mergers, the value is typically created by eliminating redundant costs or by improving the purchasing power of the combined company. In other words, when competitors merge, it's most often an exercise in cost reduction. Pretty boring stuff as the sales force goes.

However, when one company acquires another company because it has products or services that complement its own, then it becomes a very interesting story for sales. It's the story of revenue growth by cross-selling the combined company's expanded product set. Sure, there may be some cost-cutting as well, but the justification given to Wall Street is all about top-line synergy. Pretty exciting stuff for a sales force.

The assumption is that both companies will approach their existing customers with something new to sell. If you're an executive at one of the two companies, it's like instantly am-plifying the size of your sales force. You now have an entirely new group of salespeople who can begin to sell your products. And even better, the new sellers have existing relationships with customers that your old sales force doesn't know. The new sales force has access and credibility that your current sales team does not, and now they'll also have your products in their bags. Let the revenue storm begin.

This logic is what causes investors to periodically 'roll up' groups of similar companies inside an industry. If the benefits of acquiring one complementary company are good, imagine the benefits of acquiring five such companies. Or ten. Even without consolidating the companies' operations or doing much cost-reduction, the revenue to be gained by cross-selling products among the sales forces is financially compelling.

That is, of course, if you can actually accomplish the feat of cross-selling the products among all of the sales forces in your newly combined behemoth. Otherwise, you have a com-pany that's no bigger or more profitable than the sum of its parts. More importantly for the investors in the roll-up, the new behemoth is no more valu-able. In this type of investment equation, one plus one must never equal two—it must always equal three. Unfortu-nately, that kind of math is easier sold to Wall

When one company acquires another com-pany because it has products or services that complement its own, then it becomes a very interesting story for sales

Street by the bankers than to Main Street by the sales force.

THE WORST PRACTICE

Early in my consulting career, I was placed on a project working for a very large roll-up. This particular client was the combination of about 30 advertising companies. They had acquired print advertising agencies, web-design shops, distribution companies, consulting firms, and many other players in a rapidly consolidating industry. So far, so good.

The problem was that several years after the roll-up, no one was actually cross-selling the other companies' products or services. No synergies were being created, which was increasingly unacceptable to the Wall Street investors who had ponied up millions of dollars in hopes of making millions more. Enter my team of consultants.

Our job was to create sales 'playbooks' that would enable each of the company's individual business units to sell the entire range of products and services offered by the advertising conglomerate. The first phase of the project was pretty straightforward: Compile a catalogue of products and services that the aggregated sales forces could now offer. Basically, the playbooks would be a superset of the company's products, along with some basic information like product definitions, value propositions, targeted buyers, key messaging, and a list of internal contacts for the sellers to engage once a cross-selling opportunity was identified.

I was added to the team because it needed to ramp up its headcount for an avalanche of interviews to be conducted with each business unit's sales and marketing teams. As you can imagine, there was a sizeable volume of materials to be aggregated, categorized, and distilled into a tidy playbook for each of the sales forces to follow. And yet the team of consultants sat idle, waiting for the signal from the company's CEO that it was okay to commence with the interviews.

In fact, we sat idle for several weeks, waiting for the signal that never came. We busied ourselves as best we could, but we mostly just hung around the client's headquarters running up consulting fees for doing absolutely nothing but waiting. Then finally, the word came from above that the project had been cancelled by the CEO. We were to pack up our laptops and head for the parking deck. What could possibly have happened?

We learned that this project had come into direct conflict with the CEO's combative and separatist management strategy. To date, the CEO had motivated the leadership of his 30 business units in a very unique way. Each year, he would call every business unit's leader into his impressive office and scream at the cowering executive:

I've been looking at your quarterly numbers, and they're awful! You are the absolutely worst performing business unit we have! Literally, you're number 30 out of 30. I'd be embarrassed for anyone else in this company to know how terrible you are. If you don't get your <expletive> together and come back here next quarter with better numbers, you're <expletive> fired! Fired! No more second chances, I'm sick of this <expletive>! Now get out! I'll see you again in 90 days. IF I don't fire you before then.

And so it went … 30 times each year. A parade of berated executives were sent back to their silos with the fresh memory of an expletive-filled threat from the CEO. I'd like to think that the tirade at least varied from executive to executive and year to year, but I was told that the CEO pretty much stuck to his script. Truly insane leadership.

It should come as no surprise, then, that the company's revenues weren't growing. After the first few quarters, the business units had squeezed out all the improved performance they could get through the incitement of fear. The fear-mongering might have driven near-term efficiency of the sales force through greater effort, but it didn't improve effectiveness whatsoever. Our playbooks would have helped in that regard, but alas they were not to be.

When the CEO learned that our cross-selling project would necessitate improved communications among the individual business units, he cried "Halt!" He feared that if all of the executives discovered how they were truly performing against one another, his brilliant leadership strategy would be undermined. I'm not making this up. This was the stated reason that our consulting team was kicked out of the building: he didn't want us sharing information among the business units. He actively wanted to protect his silos.

Predictably, things didn't get much better for this company. It limped along for another two years before it was sold by its Wall Street investors to some other Wall Street investors. The CEO eventually made off with a big bag of money, though it would have been much bigger if he'd recognized the Worst Practice of maintaining silos between teams that need to cross-sell the others' products to succeed. Oh well. If it weren't for him, this book would be one chapter too short.

THE GOOD IDEAS

GOOD IDEA 1: COMMUNICATION ACROSS SALES TEAMS IS A GOOD THING

This is kind of obvious, but if your growth strategy is to have your sales teams cross-sell various products and services, silos are a death wish. You must do everything possible to enable each group to sell the others' wares, which includes having a clear understanding of the features, functions, value propositions, and buying processes for the complementary products. Direct communication among the sellers is a great way for them to learn—perhaps even better than formalized training.

GOOD IDEA 2: MOTIVATION CAN TAKE YOU ONLY SO FAR

It doesn't take much to motivate a sales force—at least in the near term. Whether you use a carrot or a stick, salespeople are relatively excitable. The problem is that once you get your sellers running as fast as they possibly can, motivation fails to make an incremental impact. At some point, you need to help your salespeople become better runners. Otherwise, they'll either run into a wall or run to your competitor. And that's no good for anyone.

CHAPTER SEVENTEEN

LET THE SALES FORCE FIGHT IT OUT

THE CONTEXT

How you choose to organize your sales force has a huge impact on how efficient and effective it will be. The two most basic ways to organize a sales force are to align your salespeople with certain types of customers or with certain types of products. In practice, most companies organize their sales teams in a matrix of both. This is because as a sales force grows, it makes sense for it sellers to begin to specialize in one way or another.

This specialization evolves in a pretty typical fashion. When a company hires its very first salesperson, that seller is expected to sell anything the company offers to anyone he or she can find to buy it. In other words, there is zero sales force specialization and no need to align with a particular type of customer or product. Any sale is a good sale.

However, when a sales force grows to a certain size, it makes sense to divide the sales force into smaller teams, most often aligned with different types of customers. The simplest form of customer specialization is to assign geographic territories, within which salespeople can sell to anyone. Slightly more sophisticated forms of customer alignment are to segment sellers by customer size or industry affiliation. Any way you can divide your population of targeted customers, you can align a sales force with them.

The next logical evolution of the sales force is to specialize by product type. Once a company reaches the point that it begins to offer various products and services, technical differences among the offerings demand product specialists who are familiar with each product's unique specifications. This again makes sense, and it's practically unavoidable as a company's product set grows. Customers will demand a knowledgeable seller, and no one can know everything about a complex set of products.

So what you witness in most large sales forces is the organizational result of a long history of increasing specialization. You will find sales forces that were first aligned by customer type and then further aligned with products. For instance, it would be commonplace for a manufacturing company to have an aerospace industry sales team (a customer type) that contains one group of people selling jet engines and another selling electrical components (product types). This alignment of sellers with customers and products is a good management strategy.

As I mentioned, it allows for the salespeople to develop specialized knowledge within their area of focus in order to better serve their customers. But just as importantly, it keeps the salespeople from stepping all over each other's toes. If all of your salespeople are pointed at all of your customers with all of your products in their bags, things can become pretty testy. In the absence of assigned 'territories,' salespeople attempt to stake out their own. In this situation, conflict among the salespeople is unavoidable.

Managers in organizations like this find themselves spending a lot of time mediating settlements between warring sellers. Who knew the customer first? Who identified the opportunity? Who gets the commission? Who owns the customer going forward? In the salespeople's minds, the answers to these questions determine who has won and who has lost. However, the real loser in this situation is the sellers' company,

> *Throwing your customers and products back into the general population creates a free-for-all environment that can incite a prison-yard brawl*

which has to focus its attention on internal strife rather than external prospects.

These are the reasons that every sales force tends to become increasingly specialized—both its customers and its internal stakeholders demand it. It creates order, and it makes good sense. But once you've gone down this path of dividing your sales teams into specialists, it can be tricky to unwind. Throwing your customers and products back into the general population creates a free-for-all environment that can incite a prison-yard brawl. And one of my clients was determined to learn this lesson the hard way.

THE WORST PRACTICE

I was once asked to assess the sales incentive plans for a large media company. The company had a number of cost and performance issues that it felt could be resolved if its sales force's incentives were better aligned with its corporate goals. Maybe they were right, but I've never seen a messier environment with regard to conflicting sales force objectives and behaviors. The mess was much too big to be solved by simply redesigning sales incentives, at least in my opinion.

The first thing my project team noticed was that our task was more akin to assessing the incentive plans for *several* media companies, because each of its sales forces was run completely separately from the others. Each had separate titles, separate management, separate systems, and of course, separate incentives. From the company's perspective, it was very complex.

But the situation was equally complex for the company's customers, because all of these sales forces sold to the same buyers. If you were an advertiser in a particular geographic market (say a real estate company in Los Angeles), you could potentially have four salespeople from this same media company calling on you to sell you advertising.

First you would have a rep from their Los Angeles television station calling to offer you locally televised advertising spots. Then you would have a rep from their cable network group calling to sell you advertising on nationally syndicated shows. You might also have a rep calling from the L.A. radio station that the company owned, in addition to an 'online' rep that would help you place ads the company's many Internet sites. If you wanted to advertise your real estate services in the Los Angeles market, you could spend half your life just taking sales calls from this company.

In fairness, this is also the way the sales forces in most other media companies were structured, too. It seemed reasonable at first glance, because each salesperson was a specialist with a unique product to sell from a distinct inventory of available advertising spots. However, when we dug a little deeper, we found that this strategy was not a success for anyone involved.

From the buyer's perspective, the company's marching band of salespeople had become a nuisance. Most of its customers didn't like being pestered by four or more salespeople from what was ostensibly a single company. We heard repeated customer complaints like, "Why do you need to send all of these salespeople to see me? Why can't I just deal with one person?" The buyers perceived the company's sales force as disorganized and disconnected. But some savvy customers had found a way to turn this discord to their advantage.

Though the reps sold distinct advertising products, they usually competed for the same advertising budget within the customer's marketing department. Consequently, clever customers had begun to pit the salespeople against one another to negotiate better pricing. Customers would say, "Well, I could spend $5,000 per month with you on a national network spot, but your local TV station guy is offering me something that looks pretty similar for $3,500." Literally, the company's sellers had become their own competitors.

You can see why this was so troubling to the media giant. It had hundreds of salespeople battling to capture the fluid advertising budgets of their besieged customers. But this was not an uncommon predicament, nor one that couldn't be solved. Plenty of companies gang-tackle their customers, from consulting companies with many functional specialists to technology companies with numerous product divisions. They just approach it differently.

When thoughtful companies have multiple salespeople calling on a single customer, it's a highly coordinated effort. They put guidelines in place to ensure customers (and especially large customers) get their needs met by a team of collaborative sellers who know their role in the customer relationship and how it supports a higher-level customer strategy. They have a plan, and they execute it.

Therefore, my immediate recommendation was not to redesign the sales force's incentive compensation plans, it was to define formal rules of engagement to help salespeople team up to manage their customers more proactively. Not only would the media company have more control over the products and pricing that it offered, the customers might stop complaining about the lack of coordination within the company. In my opinion, this was the first step to reining in the chaos.

However, I soon learned that my client saw things differently. In fact, the most senior executive involved in our project wanted to *loosen* the reins and kick-start the prison-yard brawl. The conversation during my final meeting with the executive team went something like this:

> *Me*: So we all agree that something needs to be done to alleviate all the conflict among your sales forces. They're beating each other up, and it's not good for you *or* your customers. As a starting point, I'd recommend putting in place some basic account planning processes and assigning a primary owner for each of your large customers. That way, there will be someone accountable for the overall growth of each customer, and the mix of products you sell to your customers can be managed more strategically.

Senior Executive: Yes, I hear what you're saying, but I'm not sure I understand why you'd want to put constraints on our salespeople. In fact, I think we might have the opposite problem. If all of our salespeople could sell any of our products, maybe they wouldn't be so protective of their own turf. Maybe they'd act in the customer's best interest and sell the bundle of products they need?

Amazingly, the executive had just entered the danger zone of a free-for-all sales force, in which any salesperson could sell any product to any customer. This strategy had never been mentioned as a potential outcome of the project, and I'll never know where he got the idea. But given the interviews we had just conducted with his salespeople and customers, I knew it was a *bad* idea.

Me: Well, based on the customer feedback we received, I'm not so sure about letting all of your salespeople sell all of your products. That could actually worsen the issue in a couple of ways. First, your customers aren't going to like the heightened feeding frenzy of your reps. But more importantly, they're going to *immediately* start playing your reps against each other, even more ruthlessly than they're doing now.

Senior Executive: Maybe. But I say we provide the incentives for our reps to sell everything we offer, and then let them fight it out. Honestly, I think we have too many salespeople in some of our markets anyway. This would weed out some of the weak performers. If I'm a customer, I think I'd like the idea of having several reps competing for my business.

Me: Okay. But to be clear, your reps would be competing with each another—to sell the exact same products to the exact same customers. Don't you think that could lead to some very deviant behaviors by your reps?

Senior Executive: If by 'very deviant' you mean 'highly motivated,' then yes. I'm sure we can put some controls into incentive plans that will keep them in line. But right now, I think this is a great way to energize our sales force and stoke our revenue engine.

At this point, several vice presidents around the table were raising their eyebrows with concern. I glanced around trying to make eye contact with anyone who would corroborate the badness of this strategy. No takers. I was on my own.

Me: As you know, we interviewed dozens of your salespeople and managers in all of your major markets. They seem to think that the competition among the sellers is already damaging their customer relationships. I can't imagine they'd welcome this new strategy. In fact, I think they would have a very negative reaction.

Senior Executive: That's just whining. If there's any friction in the field, our sales managers can work it out. That's what we pay them to do.

Me: Again, it isn't just the salespeople who are disgruntled—your customers are complaining, too. And some of them are complaining loudly. Giving sellers the incentive to more actively mob them would seem the opposite of what they want.

Senior Executive: Well, we'll never know until we give it a try. I think this is definitely what I'd like to do. Let's cut them loose and see what happens.

And that was the end of that discussion. In fact, that was the end of my involvement with the client. He adamantly wanted to go in a direction that I adamantly didn't want him to go. Nor did his sellers. Nor his customers.

I honestly don't know whether the executive's plan ever got implemented, though I seriously doubt it. There would have been a violent revolt among hundreds of salespeople if he'd tried to intensify the already contentious circumstances. I do know that their revenues remained flat for the next three years, so nothing impactful happened one way or the other. However, I'll never forget his remarkable excitement to pit his salespeople against each other and "let them fight it out." I generally wouldn't want my salespeople to fight, and certainly not with one another. And *certainly* not with their customers. But then, perhaps I'm the one who's insane.

THE GOOD IDEAS

GOOD IDEA 1: ORGANIZE YOUR SALES FORCE FOR YOUR CUSTOMERS

There's an old saying that the customer is always right. Well, of course the customer is *not* always right … but the customer is still the customer. You need to accommodate your customers, not force your will upon them, and the customers' experience begins with the way you organize your sales force around them. Be attentive to the way your customers want to be served, and serve them in that way. It will be an all-around more pleasant experience.

GOOD IDEA 2: DON'T COMPETE WITH YOURSELF

Most salespeople are competitive by nature, and their competitive drive can be a strong motivator. They compete against one another for recognition and status within the sales force, but they should never have to compete for the same customer. Some people might view such a competition as "we win either way." I view it as a "you lose either way." If there's any true winner, it might be the customer, but their victory will come with an economic and cultural cost to your company.

CHAPTER EIGHTEEN

YOU CAN HAVE A TEST DRIVE *AFTER* YOU BUY IT

THE CONTEXT

Sales processes have come a long way. Once upon a time, they were completely ignored, since sales was considered a pure art form. To even suggest that salespeople should follow a process was to limit the very freedom that made rock-star salespeople rock stars. Sales management's job was to hire the best salespeople and then stay out of their way. Any desire for rigor was effectively perceived as a sales force killer.

Then along came CRM, which promised to improve productivity in the sales force. But to accomplish this feat, leadership had to submit to the reality that selling is in fact a balance of art and science. Salespeople are actually more productive when they follow a series of consistent, repeatable steps, also known as a process. Sales management's job is still to hire the best salespeople, but now it must also provide them with a predictable path to success.

This realization has ushered in an era where great attention is paid to defining and automating relevant sales processes.

Nearly every sales force I see has invested significant time and effort in this pursuit, and it is monitored and measured with a due amount of intensity. Formal sales processes are now deeply rooted in our modern sales culture.

However, this new era of focusing on sales activities has erroneously made the salesperson the center of attention. In fact, the salesperson is not the star of the revenue-generating show, as this focus on sales process might lead you to believe. The real star suffers in the dark shadows of the mighty sales process, playing opposite the salesperson in this series of consistent, repeatable activities. The real star of this show is: the customer.

The truth that is often ignored or forgotten is that the sales process exists only as a reaction to the buying process. Buyers are in control of the selling motion, not the sellers. In fact, a salesperson's actual job is not to 'sell' anything to customer— a salesperson's job is to shepherd the customer through a buying process. Without the buying process, the sales process is irrelevant.

Furthermore, a sales process is only valuable if it closely mirrors the customer's buying process. When the two processes are misaligned, bad things happen. Salespeople spend a lot of time dutifully executing their series of selling tasks, while frustrated buyers stare at the salespeople in disbelief, wondering how the sellers can be so oblivious to their clearly stated

> *The truth that is often ignored or forgotten is that the sales process only exists as a reaction to the buying process*

needs. This disjointed process is long and painful for both participants, and the outcome is satisfying for neither.

In short, an organization can define a formal sales process, and it should. But it is the buyer's journey, and it's the buyer that is ultimately steering the sale. A salesperson can pull the buyer only so far off the buying path before both parties get lost in the wilderness. Chances are the buyer will eventually make it back onto the path and make a purchase, but it will be from the seller who stayed close to the buyer every step of the way.

THE WORST PRACTICE

I love cars. I truly believe that the act of driving is one of life's greatest pleasures. During my life I've owned big cars and small cars, fast cars and slow cars, tall cars and short cars, and I've enjoyed them all. I'm not sure why this is, though I've tried many times to explain my fascination to family and friends who are just as happy to ride in the passenger seat—a place that I despise. To me there is no riding in cars—only driving them. And this is how it is. I'm a car guy.

Consequently, purchasing a new car is a big deal for me. Not only do I have to end a close friendship with my outgoing automobile, I have to find a new car that will appreciate me for who I am. And like any new friend, the choice of a new car can't be based solely on objective data. It's a visceral decision that necessitates a face-to-face meeting and a test drive or two. Having made many new acquaintances during my car-driving years, my process for purchasing a new automobile is very well-defined and wholly inflexible. My auto-buying journey looks exactly like this:

- Step 1: *Artificially Manufacture the <u>Need</u> for a New Car*
  Regardless of how much I love my current automobile, eventually my eyes begin to wander when new technology or improved styling inevitably appears. I must then take my small grievances with the current car and build them into unbearable flaws requiring a change in equipment.
- Step 2: *Conduct Research to Narrow the Choices*
  Of course, I must do some research to understand the features and specifications of the universe of candidates. This used to require time-consuming visits to auto dealerships to collect printed brochures, but now it's done more efficiently online.
- Step 3: *Test Drive the Short List of Candidates*
  I *must* test drive every car on the short list. I have to sit in the driver's seat and experience the tactile sensations of operating the vehicle. Starting the engine, listening to the idle, accelerating, turning, and stopping. This ritual reveals the ultimate purchase criteria: how the car 'feels.'
- Step 4: *Logically Justify the Decision Already Made Emotionally*
  Invariably, the leading candidate from Step 2 fails to exhilarate in Step 3. Therefore, I need time to convince myself that the seat-of-the-pants thriller is actually a more reasonable choice than the factually superior car. This is also when I convince myself to ignore my stated budget, because no price can be placed on love.
- Step 5: *Negotiate and Purchase My New Friend*
  Finally, I feign indifference in the presence of the salesperson, and attempt to negotiate a deal that I

believe to be scandalous, though it most certainly never is. Then my new friend and I roll onto some curvy road and get to know each other a little better.

No purchase can deviate from these sequential steps in my buying process. None ever has, and none ever will. This is how it will happen, and I expect any salesperson to accommodate these steps—from providing me with information, to riding shotgun on test drives, to enduring my gestation period, and then allowing me to believe that I won the negotiation. I suspect this is a fairly common buying process, and it has rarely faced a challenge, with one noteworthy exception.

Several years ago, a completely new model of car was launched into the marketplace with great fanfare. The fanfare and critical acclaim was so great, in fact, that it immediately put me into Step 1 of my process, where I instantly manufactured significant dissatisfaction with my current automobile. Step 2 proceeded quickly as well, as I cobbled together a short list of challengers just waiting to be defeated in Step 3—the test drive. And this is where things went unimaginably wrong.

I strode confidently into the car dealership, ready for my test drive. I stood casually but purposefully just inside the front door waiting for a salesperson to approach. As the smiling young man extended his hand, the conversation proceeded something like this:

Salesperson: Hello, sir, how are you doing?

Me: I'm doing great, thank you.

Salesperson: How can I help you today?

Me: I'd like to test drive the <insert cool new car>.

Salesperson: That's great. Are you going to buy that car today?

Me (startled by his direct question): I'm sorry?

Salesperson: I asked if you are ready to buy the car today.

Me: Well, probably not today. I'm also looking at other cars. (Already feigning indifference, in preparation for our impending negotiation.)

Salesperson: Well, we have only a couple of those cars, and they're way in the back of the lot. I don't think we can get one of those out for a test drive. (These were his exact words.)

Me (confused): What?

Salesperson: Yeah, they're way back there. There are a lot of other cars on the lot, and the model you're looking for is pretty much trapped behind them. We can't take one out for you to test drive.

Me: (silence)

Salesperson: (silence)

Me (deciding to start over): So I'm very interested in that car, and I'd like to take it for a drive today.

Salesperson: Well … as I said, we have only a couple and they're way in the back of the lot. Unless, of course, you're willing to purchase one today.

Me: So you're telling me that you will not let me drive that car unless I first agree to buy it? That's what you're telling me?

Salesperson: Yes, that's what I'm saying.

I stood there for what seemed like an hour, staring at him staring back at me. And then I turned without saying a word and went back to my car, where I sat in my car replaying the conversation and becoming increasingly annoyed. I then got out of my car, walked back into the dealership, and breezed right past that same salesperson (who had his hand extended toward me as though he had not just met me ten minutes earlier). I walked a straight line to the first person I could find sitting behind a desk and said:

Me: I'd like to speak to a sales manager, please.

Sales Manager: I'm the sales manager. How can I help you?

Me: Yes, I'd like to test drive the <elusive new car>.

Sales Manager: That's great. Do you think you might want to buy that car today?

Me (staring at him staring at me): Well, I'm not sure, but I'd like to take one for a drive.

Sales Manager: Yeah, we only have a couple of those models, and they're way in the back of the lot. I don't think we can get one out for a test drive. Unless you're pretty sure you want to buy one today.

Me (fuming): Well, I can't tell you that I'm going to buy one today, but I can *promise* you that I will *not* buy one unless I drive it first.

Sales Manager: I don't think we can do that for you.

Me: So you'd rather send me away than let me drive that car?

Sales Manager: No, I'd much rather sell you the car. But otherwise, yes.

I returned to my car where I sat for several more minutes, half expecting the manager and salesperson to come running out with a camera crew laughing at the farce. I also suspected that a giant hole might open up beneath my car and suck me back into the universe where I had previously learned the laws of buying and selling. When neither of those things happened, I put my car in drive and proceeded to another car dealership in a nearby city. Now I was on a mission to drive this car.

I walked into the next dealership somewhat less confidently, but nevertheless I asked the salesperson who approached me:

Me: Hi. I'd like to test drive the <most elusive car ever manufactured>.

Salesperson: That's great. Are you hoping to buy that car today?

Me: You know, it's funny that you should say that. I was just at another dealership, and they asked me the very same question right before I walked out the door. Twice. What's going on here?

Salesperson (leaning toward me and speaking quietly): Well, that's a *really* popular car right now, and we've had a lot of people coming in just to take it for a joy ride. It's wasting a lot of our salespeople's time, so management told us we're not allowed to let people test drive it unless they can convince us that they're serious about buying it.

Me: So people are coming in here and buying those cars without ever driving them? Without even seeing them?

Salesperson: One or two people have, yes.

Me: Well, that's great. And I might also buy one. But I will *never* buy a car that I don't test drive first.

Salesperson (looking around nervously): I know, it's crazy. Alright. Stay here, and I'll be back in five minutes with one for you to drive. If my manager happens to walk by, tell him that you came here to buy it.

And so I finally drove the car. Sadly, I didn't even like it. Despite all of its praise and acclaim, it was no fun to drive. At least not for me. Someone once told me that you don't get to choose who you fall in love with. I guess that also applies to cars.

But that morning was not wasted. Out of it came the most perfect example ever of misaligned buying and selling processes. One participant in the process wanted to drive it before he'd buy it, and the other wanted to sell it before he'd drive it. Most amazingly, this dysfunctional sales process was architected by sales management. They made the insane decision to purposefully erect a barrier to buying.

Fortunately, the second salesperson was smart enough to recognize the misalignment and adapt his sales process to accommodate my buying process. He realized that the buyer was in control and that his manager's directive didn't make any sense. Alas, he didn't make the sale, because the product didn't fit my need. But at least he had a chance.

THE GOOD IDEAS

GOOD IDEA 1: THE SELLING PROCESS MUST MIRROR THE BUYING PROCESS

Sales forces are fixated on sales processes and the consistent execution of sales activities ... and they should be. However, they shouldn't forget that the real task of a salesperson is to help a buyer buy. If your selling activities are misaligned with the buying activities on the other side of the handshake, then you're placing unnecessary obstacles in the way. Start with the buying process and build your selling process backward from there. Then sales will happen on a natural course.

GOOD IDEA 2: THE BUYER IS IN CONTROL—ALWAYS

Salespeople are expected to be aggressive. Sometimes that's a good thing, because it gives sellers the confidence to drive a sale forward. But sometimes it's a bad thing, because it gives sellers the false sense that they are in control of the buyer's decision-making process. The buyer is *always* in control of the decision-making process, because she's the only one who can decide to buy. Ignore this fact at your own economic peril.

CHAPTER NINETEEN

MOTIVATION THROUGH FAILURE

THE CONTEXT

Sales management spends a lot of time trying to motivate salespeople. Unfortunately, this can create an outsized sense of urgency that emphasizes short-term activity over the achievement of long-term goals. And management can fall into the trap of relying on incentives as a replacement for good, attentive management. But make no mistake—motivation is extremely important to the sales force.

Of course, motivation is not exclusively for salespeople. From the factory floor to the executive suite, you'll find rewards, recognition, and incentive plans everywhere you look. Which makes sense. You want your employees to come to work every morning with a desire to do well, and acknowledging good performance is a very powerful way to keep a strong wind in your employees' sails.

If you break down any incentive program to its most basic components, there are two fundamental pieces. First there is the *performance target*. This is the level of achievement at which the worker's productivity is declared a 'success.' For a factory worker, this might be fabricating 15 units per hour, or for a marketing executive, it might be achieving a 25% market share. Of course, the most

> *What you absolutely do not want to do is screw up your incentives so badly that you actually demotivate your sales team*

typical performance target for salespeople is to accrue a certain level of sales revenue per year—also known as their quota. Whether it's $50 thousand or $5 million, salespeople know exactly what level of performance represents success.

The second component of an incentive system is pretty obvious—the *incentive itself*. This is the reward that workers receive if they meet their performance targets. The incentive for a sales force is most often a cash payment, but it need not be. I've seen salespeople who were extremely motivated by all types of non-cash incentives, such as trophies, medallions, rings, and certificates. Just being recognized as a success has its own intrinsic value.

There are many other considerations in administering an incentive program, such as the mechanisms by which performance is calculated, the process of setting objectives, and the timing of the actual rewards. But in general, you can motivate your salespeople successfully if they simply know what they need to do and what they'll receive if they do it.

What you absolutely do *not* want to do is screw up your incentives so badly that you actually *demotivate* your sales team. During my career I've seen pretty much every possible way to design a suboptimal incentive system, but most of the time the blunders were benign enough that they didn't completely destroy the integrity of the program. However, there is one particular instance of poor incentive plan design that was not only devastating in its badness—it was intentionally perpetrated by the company's executive leadership.

THE WORST PRACTICE

I was hired by a high tech manufacturing company to perform a general assessment of its sales force. Unlike most of my consulting projects where there was a specifically known problem that needed to be resolved, my client was just generally displeased with the performance of its sales force. The company had not reached its revenue growth goals for several years, and the head of sales was on a short leash to get things into shape.

We were in the process of conducting sales leadership team interviews, during which we were asking a variety of questions about the sales force's organizational structure, selling roles, sales processes, enabling technology, compensation plans, and other topics. You never know what will come out of these interviews, and they're usually uneventful fact-finding excursions. But once in a while you hear something that is easily identifiable as a serious problem. For example:

Speaking with the company's director of sales operations, I opened our conversation with a big-picture question.

Me: I understand that your sales force's performance has been disappointing for the last few years. I'd be interested to hear your opinion of what's going on. Do you think it's an issue with the skills of the salespeople, or is there something else that's holding them back?

Director: Well, I don't think it's a lack of skill that's the problem. Our salespeople are actually pretty talented and experienced. In fact, I worked for one of our competitors prior to taking this role, and I'd say that our sales force here is of higher caliber than our competition's.

Me: So if they are both talented and experienced, why are they struggling?

Director: Honestly, I don't think they're very motivated to succeed.

Me: That's an interesting thing to say. Why wouldn't they be motivated? I've seen their compensation plans, and they look pretty generous.

Director: Yes, they would be *quite* generous, if anybody ever achieved quota.

Me: What do you mean?

Director: No salespeople ever make their quotas.

Me: No salespeople ever make their quotas? Like … None of them?

Director: No. I've been here three years, and no salesperson has ever reached his or her quota during that time. So they never get the big incentive payouts.

Me [squinting]: Umm. Why don't they reach their quota?

Director: Because their quotas are set ridiculously high. It would be virtually impossible for anyone to reach them.

Me [now with my head tilted slightly]: Why are they so high? Who sets them?

Director: The CEO of the company. For some reason, he thinks that salespeople shouldn't reach their quotas. He believes sellers are only motivated if they have something to reach for, so he sets these ridiculous goals for them.

Me [now blinking rapidly]: Huh.

Director [shrugging her shoulders]: Yeah, I know.

Me: Well, I've never heard of that before. But what you're telling me is that his plan isn't working. It's actually backfiring.

Director: Yes, the salespeople are actually *demotivated* in my opinion. Obviously we've discussed this many times, but the CEO is adamant that this is the way he wants the compensation plans structured. I don't see it changing anytime soon.

Me: Then I'm not sure I see the company's sales results changing anytime soon.

Director: No. Me neither.

In a subsequent interview, the head of sales identified the same issue as a major barrier to success, though he expressed it with a much higher degree of frustration. He knew that it was a bad management strategy to try to motivate salespeople by assuring their failure. No matter how rich the incentive, it's not motivational if the target is completely out of reach.

In the end, we proposed implementing some cash-based sales contests and other non-cash incentives to create some carrots that were actually edible. But what a mess it was. I never spoke to the company's resident expert in motivation— the CEO—so I really don't know what he was thinking. But I'd wager that he never held a sales role, or else he'd have realized the folly of his strategy. I'd also wager that his own compensation plan was a little more forgiving than those of his sellers, and that he got a nice bonus every single year.

As a rule of thumb, you should set your sales targets such that two-thirds of your salespeople achieve their quotas. This ensures that your solid performers get to taste success, and those who don't still view their goals as attainable in the future. Regardless, it's a definite Worst Practice to doom all of your salespeople to failure, including your top performers. When you start a race that you know you won't finish, you tend to do a lot of walking along the way.

THE GOOD IDEAS

GOOD IDEA 1: SET YOUR SALES TARGETS CAREFUL-LY

Sales targets can be set in a number of ways, from the top-down allocation of the company's target to field-level negotiations between sellers and their managers. However you choose to go about it, make sure your salespeople's performance targets are viewed as achievable. You want to motivate your sellers to high levels of performance, but you don't want to set them on a path to assured failure. When targets are set properly, your top performers will reach them and your bottom performers won't. But they should nevertheless be motivated to try.

GOOD IDEA 2: CREATE A CULTURE OF SUCCESS

People like to succeed, and success is contagious. Don't be afraid to feed a culture of success by setting your sellers up to win. And when they do, celebrate their victories loudly. Once your salespeople's sails are full of wind, they'll tend to pick up speed, and the resulting revenue regatta will be a beautiful thing to watch. It sure beats watching your fleet of boats sitting dead in the water, with no wind in the forecast.

CHAPTER TWENTY

I DON'T NEED BABYSITTERS

THE CONTEXT

Once upon a time, salespeople were lone wolves. As late as the nineteenth century, 'peddlers' and 'drummers' loaded up their horse-drawn wagons and journeyed into the American frontier to sell their wares to remote households and local storefronts. They were both the manufacturer's sales force and its distribution channel. They left home with a bunch of stuff and returned when the stuff was gone. One man, one wagon, and one goal: empty the wagon.

Then in the early twentieth century, large corporate sales forces began to appear. Led by innovative leaders like John Henry Patterson at National Cash Register and then Thomas Watson at IBM, companies began to assemble the sales organizations that are familiar to us today. Their companies hired thousands of professional salespeople with formal job descriptions, assigned territories, training classes, incentive programs, and quotas. The lone wolves became a pack. And to help lead and direct these groups of professional sellers, companies created sales managers.

Today sales managers play an invaluable role in the operation of a sales force. In fact, the role is so multi-faceted that it's difficult to succinctly describe. Sales managers are the intersection of many functions inside an organization, connecting field sales with executive leadership, marketing, finance, manufacturing, IT, and every other nook within the company. But unquestionably the most important role of sales managers is still to manage their frontline sellers.

Sales managers are therefore the leaders of the pack. Salespeople may not necessarily want their sales managers to follow them around nonstop, but they sure want their managers to remove internal barriers, resolve customer issues, and fight for their commissions. They expect their managers to communicate important information, shelter them from the mundane, and procure the resources to help them succeed.

In short, sales managers are the glue that holds a sales force together. Without sales managers, you would see a far-flung collection of independent agents, most of whom would perform below their potential. With no one to communicate, coordinate, and calibrate their performance, salespeople would fail to continually grow their capabilities. Many would find a comfortable orbit and remain there indefinitely. With no clear career path and no internal advocate, sellers would live much less inspired

> *Without sales managers, you would see a far-flung collection of independent agents, most of whom would perform below their potential*

lives. So sales managers matter. A lot.

It's therefore remarkable to me that sales managers don't receive more recognition than they do. It's a truly uncelebrated role compared to the rainmakers below them and the executives above. They remain sandwiched in the middle of the organization and unceremoniously keep the wheels of their sales forces turning. As long as sales managers keep doing their jobs, sellers tend to blossom and things move along just fine. But when they suddenly disappear, things predictably start to go haywire.

THE WORST PRACTICE

I received a strange call one day from the vice president of marketing at a mid-sized manufacturer. Foremost, it was unusual for a marketing executive to be the first person to contact me from a potential client. I often end up working with marketing teams, but only because my work with their sales forces requires me to collaborate for very specific purposes.

Secondly, it was strange because the woman began to ask me for insights and guidance on issues that were very squarely in the sales management domain—areas like sales process, sales metrics, sales coaching, and organization structure. Her questions were so broad-based and rudimentary that it sounded as if someone had just handed her a large sales force to run, and she had no idea where to begin. Finally I inquired:

Me: These are some very interesting questions that you're asking. Are you planning to hire a sales force that would report to you?

Marketing Executive: No, we already have a sales force. We have about 100 salespeople, including some technical support staff.

Me: So do you oversee both the marketing *and* the sales functions?

Executive: No, I lead only the marketing group, which is around ten people. I'm just trying to exert some influence over the sales force, since we're having some very serious issues over there.

Me: What kind of issues?

Executive: Well, there's absolutely no discipline to what the salespeople are doing. Everyone's pretty much doing his own thing, which is working for some people, but most of our reps are really struggling to hit their quotas. And that's leading to issues with our customers, because salespeople are starting to target each other's accounts. Generally, morale is very low and going lower.

Me: Geez. That doesn't sound like a good situation.

Executive: No, it's not. It's a real mess, actually, and it's only getting worse.

Me: I don't mean to question your role in this. We've been chatting for only 15 minutes, and I don't presume to know your organizational dynamics. But isn't your sales management team worried about this? Shouldn't they be the ones trying to get this all under control?

Executive: Yes, but we don't have a sales management team.

Me: Excuse me?

Executive: We don't have any sales managers. That's part of the problem.

Me: Perhaps I misunderstood. Are your salespeople independent agents, like manufacturer's reps who work for themselves and represent your products along with other suppliers?

Executive: No, all of the salespeople are direct employees of our company.

Me: Well ... [processing]... if you have 100 salespeople who work for your company, why don't you have any sales managers to lead them?

Executive: Our CEO fired them all.

Me: [silence; unable to process]

Executive: [silence; waiting for me to process]

Me: When?

Executive: About two years ago.

Me: But ... why did your CEO fire your entire sales management team?

Executive: He didn't think we needed them. In fact, his exact words were, "My salespeople are all adults, and they have very rich commission plans. If they're good at what they do, they'll make a lot of money and be happy. If they're bad, they'll fail and leave. Why do I need a bunch of 'managers' to sit around and babysit my salespeople?" So he gave all of our sales mangers the choice to become sales reps or be fired. About half became reps, and the other half went to competitors. *Technically* we do have a VP of Sales, but he just creates sales forecasts and manages a few large accounts.

Me: Huh.

Executive: Yeah, it was a really dumb thing to do, but the CEO was adamant that the sales managers were just an administrative cost. And in fairness, everything was going okay for the first six months or so, but then it all started to spiral out of control.

Me: That doesn't surprise me.

Executive: No, it didn't surprise me either. The only thing that *is* surprising is that the CEO still hasn't changed his mind. He thinks this chaos is just "a part of the process," but I know we have to do something to help these poor salespeople. They're flailing about and really in need of direction.

Me: Well, I appreciate what you're trying to do. And I think you're asking all of the right questions. The problem is going to be that these salespeople don't report to you.

Executive: I know. And I'm not sure how much influence I can actually exert before the CEO notices what I'm doing. But we can't have a sales force with no oversight. Two more years like this, and we might all lose our jobs. Just like our 'babysitters' did two years ago.

I've seen a lot of crazy things in my career, but I have to admit that this one shocked me. As a rule, management is a good thing. This is true in any part of a company, but I think it's particularly important in the sales force.

Most salespeople are already on the fringe of their organizations, because they work in the field and focus their attention outward toward customers. Without someone to engage, organize, and guide their efforts, they risk becoming lone wolves once again. And as this woman clearly explained, lone wolves often find themselves attacking one another and damaging their ecosystem.

Though I've never seen a company fire its sales managers outright, I have worked with many companies where the role of the sales manager was minimized. Sometimes sales management is viewed as the place where mediocre sellers go to die. Other times, sales managers' spans of control are so large (say, 20 salespeople to a manager) that they can effectively do nothing more than generate reports and monitor troublemakers. But even in these suboptimal situations, there's still a pack leader controlling the effort. No modern company should run its sales forces using a nineteenth-century sales model.

THE GOOD IDEAS

GOOD IDEA 1: SALESPEOPLE SHOULD NOT BE TREATED AS LONE WOLVES

Many salespeople like to think of themselves as lone wolves, but in reality they tend to be more successful when they work in a pack. Organizational and marketplace dynamics are increasingly complicated, and sellers that don't communicate or collaborate will develop large blind spots. They'll bounce around and nip at each other until the lack of coordination creates a sales force that equals less than the sum of its parts. But when sellers operate as a cohesive team to share insights and resources, everyone is much more likely to prosper.

GOOD IDEA 1: SALES MANAGERS MATTER ... A LOT

Sales managers are the leaders of the pack, and they keep their individual sellers healthy, wealthy, and wise. They have the unique ability to corral and coordinate team members and to apply organizational resources where needed. A good sales management team is worth its weight in gold, because it drives greater productivity across the entire sales force. Discount your sales managers and you will be discounting your team's performance. Celebrate your managers, and you will be toasting to your future success.

CHAPTER TWENTY-ONE

DO WE HAVE THOSE COMPENSATION PLANS YET?

I could write an entire series of books on nothing but the insanity I've seen surrounding sales compensation. In fact, I've exercised restraint to limit the number of compensation-related vignettes in this book. Therefore, indulge my slightly longer narrative in this chapter. There is much to say on this topic, and I have a perfect story to capture some representative madness.

THE CONTEXT

Sales compensation plans are uniquely disastrous in many sales forces. More than any other part of the sales ecosystem, a bad compensation plan can poison the water and air that would otherwise sustain a healthy selling environment. The worst part is that sales compensation plans—and especially the bad ones—are often concocted with great management care and attention. The damage that they inflict is therefore deliberate, even if unintended.

In fact, toxic sales compensation plans can be the product of substantial organizational effort. The desire to get compensation plans 'right' can lead management to hire external consultants, form large internal design teams, and endure prolonged projects. Yet the more time organizations spend churning out the next compensation schemes, the more convoluted and calamitous they seem to become.

How is it that such well-intentioned effort could yield such counterproductive output? Is sales compensation itself an insane actor in the sales force's story? No, not exactly. But sales compensation suffers from a characteristic that makes it highly susceptible to both substantial effort and convoluted design: It is the single sales management decision that receives extreme levels of attention from *both* salespeople and their managers. Let's look at sales compensation from each of these perspectives to see why it's so important and why it can go so wrong.

Compensation from the Sellers' Perspective

Salespeople tend to pay more attention to their compensation plans than any other aspect of their jobs. Do they care which CRM tool management purchases? Maybe. Do they care which phone service their company uses? Perhaps. Would they ever quit their jobs over either of those decisions? No. But we've all seen sellers quit over their compensation plans.

Sellers care intensely about their compensation plans for two understandable reasons. First, compensation is very personal. The amount of money you make has a direct impact on the life you lead, since it can influence everything from your family's lifestyle to your own self-esteem. When you take home less compensation than you think you deserve, it has an immediate and noteworthy effect on your personal wellbeing.

The more time organizations spend churning out the next compensation schemes, the more convoluted and calamitous they seem to become

Second, compensation is a tangible measure of success or failure, because it is objectively quantifiable. If someone were to ask you how satisfied you are with your job, you'd probably respond with a subjectively vague answer. And if they subsequently asked you to rank your satisfaction relative to your peers, your response would be similarly vague, because it's impossible to know exactly where you stand on some universal scale of satisfaction.

However, if someone asked you how much compensation you received last year, you'd know the exact amount. Unlike your satisfaction with your job, your financial rewards are explicit. And if you're like most salespeople, you'd also know precisely how your compensation compared to that of your peers. Because compensation is so personal and quantifiable, sellers pay very close attention to it.

Compensation from Management's Perspective

Sales management also cares intensely about compensation plans. Of course they understand how important they are for the reasons mentioned above—they too were salespeople once upon a time. Management wants to make its compensation plans both generous and equitable, so it can attract and retain the best sales talent.

But sales management also has other objectives for sales compensation, and this is where the messiness begins. Management incites insanity when it tries to use compensation plans to accomplish too many things. I'll share with you three of management's most common goals for its sales compensation plans—two that make total sense and a third that creates the madness.

The first goal is by far the most important and useful, which is to create an *incentive* for sellers to do the right things. This is, in fact, why the variable portion of a salesperson's compensation is usually called an incentive plan. When the plan is designed well, sellers' effort is pointed in the right direction. If a sales compensation plan did *nothing* more than properly motivate salespeople, it would be an unquestionable success in my mind.

The second management goal for compensation plans is also a legitimate use, which is to *reward* good performance. When sellers achieve their individual objectives, they contribute to the success of the overall company. Their compensation plans should then recognize this contribution by sharing the spoils of their work. Though companies often fail to differentiate the two goals of offering an incentive and providing a reward, both are still clever things to do.

The third management objective is the chief offender in most compensation crimes. This is the desire to use compensation to *police* bad behaviors by salespeople. Stated differently, sales compensation plans are often used as 'managers in absentia' to discourage salespeople from misbehaving while their managers aren't watching. Examples would be plans that punish sellers for timing their sales to maximize commissions or for poaching customers from another salesperson's territory. These are, of course, bad behaviors that you want to discourage, but not necessarily through a compensation plan.

Trying to police salespeople's behaviors through a compensation plan not only demonstrates a lack of trust and alignment in your sales force, it can complicate the plans beyond the bounds of common sense. If you find an over-engineered compensation plan, you can be sure there is police work embedded somewhere in it. My obvious advice: Limit the role of compensation to incentives and rewards, and forget about compensation as law-enforcement device.

In sum, good sales compensation design is a critical determinant of a well-run sales force. It is justifiably important to both salespeople and sales management, though for different reasons. When you get sales compensation right, sellers feel motivated and rewarded, and their behaviors are aligned with your organization's goals. Life is good for everyone involved. But when you get compensation wrong ...

THE WORST PRACTICE

I received a call one March from a human resource director at a software firm. She explained that the VP of sales in one of the company's divisions wanted to redesign his team's compensation plan, and she needed a consultant to assist with the task. None of this seemed odd, except that this type of call typically comes in September or October as organizations are planning for the upcoming year. I thought to myself, "Wow, these folks are really on top of next year's compensation plan." But no.

The woman revealed that they were just starting to design their *current* year's incentive plan—the year that was already under way. When I asked about the delayed timing, she was remarkably unconcerned. "This is just how it happens here," she said. "Our salespeople get year-end bonuses based on their full-year performance, so it's not important to have it all figured out at the beginning of the year."

I expressed apprehension that the sales team was currently working away with no idea what they were working toward, but again, she was indifferent. "Trust me, they're used to it. Our sales leader is always very focused on getting the sales force's compensation plans perfect, and this is just a part of the process." It was easy for me to see that they were off to a bad start.

Mercifully, she *did* feel a sense of urgency to remedy this situation, so I agreed to engage immediately and help her team design new incentive plans. Shortly afterward, I was discussing the state of affairs with their VP of sales.

> *Me*: I understand that you want to redesign your bonus plan for this year. Can I ask what specifically you don't like about last year's plan?

> *Sales Leader*: As always, there were some bad behaviors in the sales force last year that we need to address using this year's incentives. We need to redesign the parameters so that my salespeople don't misbehave.

> *Me*: What kind of misbehaviors are you talking about?

> *Sales Leader*: Well, there are a lot of little things they do that really annoy me, but the biggest thing is that they try to game the system to maximize their bonuses, so our year-end payouts tend to be very rich.

Me: Well a little bit of 'gaming' is to be expected. Any time you give salespeople an incentive compensation plan, they're going to reverse-engineer it to find out how they can make the most money. But then, that's actually the point of an incentive plan—to get your salespeople doing what you want them to do. You *need* them to see through the plan design and know your intentions.

Sales Leader: Maybe so. But I *need* them to know that they *need* to stop gaming their bonuses. I want to add some stuff into this year's plan that will be punitive for their bad behavior and bring their bonuses back in line.

Me: So rather than an incentive plan, you actually want a *dis*-incentive plan?

Sales Leader: I guess you could characterize it that way.

Me: Okay. But in my professional opinion, the purpose of compensation should be to provide incentives and re-wards, not to punish sellers. Don't you find it a little counterintuitive to use an incentive plan for punishment?

Sales Leader: No. The incentive plan is the most powerful management tool I have, because salespeople pay *total* at-tention to it. I think it's the *best* way to discourage bad behaviors, in fact. We just need to make sure it addresses all of the potential problems.

Realizing that I would lose a head-to-head battle with this sales force's police chief, I decided to retreat from the fight and take the pulse of his sales team. I left his office certain that I would find a field full of anxious salespeople and managers fretting nervously over their uncertain financial futures. But this sales force offered nothing but surprises.

I interviewed several sales managers to understand the impact of these perpetually delayed and potentially punitive incentive plans. My first conversation went something like this:

> *Me*: I was speaking with your vice president earlier this week, and he feels pretty strongly that last year's bonus plan was encouraging some deviant behaviors by your sellers. More specifically, he seems to think that your salespeople spend a lot of time gaming the system to maximize their bonuses.

> *Sales Manager*: Yeah, that sounds like him. He loves to focus on the bonus plan. But I can promise you that our salespeople aren't gaming it. Our bonus plan is so complex, I don't know how any salesperson *could* game it. There are probably a dozen different incentives for doing certain things, and then there are ways the compensation actually gets *reduced* for other reasons. The whole thing is ridiculous. I couldn't explain it to you in an hour if I tried.

> *Me*: Hmm. Well, he says the sellers are getting really big payouts every year, which I think is leading him to conclude that they're gaming the system.

> *Sales Manager*: No, the reason the salespeople get big bonuses every year is because their direct supervisors, like me, have the ability to override the guidelines and pay bonuses however we see fit.

Me: I'm sorry? I don't think I understand.

Sales Manager: The incentive structure is so absurd that it's not really fair to pay our salespeople according to it. Our people work really hard, and they do a great job for our company. If we actually paid the bonuses strictly according to the plan, the payouts would be completely random. We'd have rock stars getting low bonuses and our worst sellers making off like bandits. I'd lose my best sellers within a year or two, for sure.

Me: So you're completely ignoring the design of the compensation plans?

Sales Manager: Well, yes and no. Yes, I'm ignoring the specific calculations of the bonuses, but I think I'm following the spirit of the plan, which is to reward good performance. I mean, the salespeople go the first half of every year without even having an incentive plan. I'm just trying to make it all fair for my folks.

I went on to interview several salespeople who confirmed that they had no idea how their bonuses were actually calculated, and they generally just trusted their managers to do the right thing. In fact, their attitude toward their bonus plan was summed up by one seller who commented, "Honestly, I don't pay that much attention to it during the year. It always seems to work itself out in the end."

As you can tell from these conversations, this company's incentive plan was useless. If the goal was to inspire or discourage certain behaviors, it failed. If the goal was to recognize top performers, it failed. And it failed predictably, because several bad management decisions had reduced it to little more than a sales force nuisance.

First, the company perennially published its incentive plans halfway through the year. Even if they were the best-designed plans ever, they'd still have only half the desired impact, because the sales force was rudderless for six months at a time. Rather than starting the year with clear goals in sight, the salespeople were conditioned to just work hard and hope for the best.

Second, they clearly *weren't* the best-designed plans ever, because they failed to guide performance. In an attempt to create incentive plans that would motivate (and police) every possible behavior, the company created plans so complex that they amounted to white noise. They distorted the salespeople's vision, rather than helping to sharpen it.

Ultimately, this sales force's 'incentive' compensation plans were no greater a management tool than any other discretionary bonus awarded to any other employee in the world. In fact, I suspect its salespeople's motivation would have been identical if they'd had no incentive whatsoever, and the salespeople simply received a salary based on their prior year's performance. As annual incentive compensation plans go, this one started off on one bad foot and ended on the other.

THE GOOD IDEAS

GOOD IDEA 1: COMPENSATION PLANS MUST WORK
FOR BOTH SALESPEOPLE AND MANAGEMENT

Compensation is extremely important to everyone in the sales force. For salespeople, it represents success, prosperity, and stature. For management, it serves to align, motivate, and reward. When designing a sales compensation plan, both perspectives are critical to consider. Treat it purely as remuneration for sellers, and you lose the ability to guide the sales force. Treat it purely as a control mechanism for management, and you lose the ability to inspire performance. Balance both, and you'll have a sales team that will run really hard in precisely the right direction.

GOOD IDEA 2: DON'T OVER-ENGINEER SALES COMPENSATION

When designing compensation plans, most sales leaders struggle with simplicity. It's easy to jam more and more stuff into a compensation plan, assuming that your salespeople will heed the various signals and give you all the things you want. But the exact opposite is true. The more objectives you squeeze into a compensation plan, the more noise you broadcast to the field. Eventually, your salespeople will recognize it as such and begin to tune it out.

GOOD IDEA 3: INCENTIVE COMPENSATION SHOULD MOTIVATE AND REWARD, NOT PUNISH

The reason that incentive plans aren't called dis-incentive plans is kind of obvious: They're meant to inspire good performance, not to censure bad behavior. If you want to discourage petty crimes in your sales force, do so through rigorous sales management and disciplinary action. If you want to drive sales results, do so through clear direction and generous rewards. Attempting to do both through a single compensation plan sends mixed signals and dampens the very enthusiasm that you're trying to create.

CHAPTER TWENTY-TWO

YOUR MATH IS WRONG!

THE CONTEXT

Salespeople and their managers are not the best mathematicians. In fact, it's fairly common for even the most basic mathematical equations to yield completely unexpected results in the sales force. It's not because salespeople are poorly educated or unintelligent—to the contrary, research shows that people who work in sales are much more educated than the general population. And it's not that Excel or calculators don't work in the hands of salespeople—they function just as well as they do in the hands of engineers or financiers.

Rather, the sales force suffers from something akin to perpetual wishful thinking. In such a world, numbers tend to get stretched in one direction or the other with little regard to the otherwise immutable rules of math. Numbers get pushed, pulled, rounded (up or down), chopped, boosted, and even outright ignored if the conclusions don't suit the desired outcomes of the person punching the keys on the tabulation machine.

For instance, in the rest of the world $1 million is generally accepted to equal $1 million dollars. However, if a salesperson were forecast a $1 million deal to her manager, it might suddenly become $1.25 million if the manager's own forecast is falling a little short. Or if the manager happens to feel rather confident that the revenue

> *It's fairly common for even the most basic mathematical equations to yield completely unexpected results in the sales force*

forecast is already assured for the quarter, that deal might suddenly become $750,000. You see, $1 million might actually represent a range of values in the sales force, depending on the circumstance.

Time can also fall victim to murky math in the hands of sales. For instance, a buyer might tell a salesperson that a pending purchase will occur in 90 days. Now to the seller, that 90 days might actually mean 120 days or 60 days, depending on how the salesperson is tallying numbers at the moment. And by the time that interval makes it to the input screen of CRM, time might have further slowed or accelerated. Concrete numbers become abstract suggestions when they enter the domain of sales.

And the abstractions don't just relate to forecasts and deals—there are metrics of all types at work in sales forces. From headcount, to sales calls, to discounts, and close rates, nearly everything that can be measured in a sales force is measured. CRM and sales force automation have provided us with that ability. Yet numbers still seem to get bent, qualified, minimized, or maximized, depending on the need.

Making this phenomenon even more remarkable, sales is held accountable to those numbers. It's not as if no one will question what happened to that $1.25 million deal 120 days later. Or the $750,000 deal 60 days later. There is extensive reporting in the sales force that should capture and expose the fundamental breakdown of mathematical laws. However, that never seems to happen, because the sales force will have already moved on to its next blurry equation. That is, until all the fuzzy math eventually piles up, and the day of reconciliation arrives.

THE WORST PRACTICE

I was hired by a manufacturer to help it transform its sales force. The company had been distributing its products in North America for decades, but it could not get its market share higher than third place. Being the number three player meant that it often resorted to price concessions to win deals, which left its profit margins among the lowest in the industry. The executive team believed that the sales force was the issue, since its products were well-regarded and performed well in independent quality tests.

The objective of the transformation was to realign the North American sales force with some new industry segments that its marketing department had defined. The hope was that by aligning the company's sales resources more closely with its customers, it would be easier for the sales team to differentiate its products and to gain market share. The VP of North American sales had recruited me to help because of some similar work I had done for another division of the company.

At its core, this was nothing more than a territory design project, which is a mathematical exercise. We needed to identify all of the customer segments, locate those customers on a map, determine what level of service each segment required, and then calculate where the company's sales reps should be located and in what quantity. For instance, if there were 200 customers of a particular type in the New York market, and each sales rep could service 100 customers, then the New York market needed two sales reps for that segment. No problem; it's just math.

As I began working with the team, it was pointed out to me that the company's sales force was substantially smaller than its competition's. I began to hear things like, "Competitor A has a *very* inefficient sales force. Where we have one sales rep, they have three. That's why our cost of sale is so much lower than theirs." Or a different variation on the theme, "Our sales reps work much harder than the competition's. We can cover nearly twice as much geographic territory as they can with the same number of salespeople."

While both of these facts might have been true, it was unquestionable that my client was number three in the market. And the top two led by a considerable margin. It didn't take long before I began to suspect that its team was just too small to accomplish its market share objectives. But my personal suspicions were irrelevant, because we would be using mathematics to determine what headcount was appropriate for the sales force. My guesses were no better than their sales management's. In fact, I would have deferred to management's judgment, since they were living and breathing this issue every single day. If things were really out of whack in the field, I assumed that they would have known it. But then this book is filled with bad assumptions.

I spent several weeks interviewing salespeople, managers, sales operations, and marketing to understand the new customer segments and the level of effort required to service and sell to each. We then collaborated to vet the assumptions one by one, again and again, so that everyone on the project team felt comfortable with the eventual inputs to our territory coverage model. Ultimately, everyone agreed to which type of customer should receive what level of effort in what measure from each sales role. And then, I let our territory mapping software do the math.

The math revealed that in almost every region of North America the company's sales force needed to double in size. Double. If one region had six salespeople, it needed twelve. If the region had one sales support person, it needed two. If two sales engineers, then four. Across the entire organization, top to bottom, the sales force was undersized by 50% to achieve its market share objectives.

This conclusion even stood up to a marketplace reality check. Its next biggest competitor (number two in market share) had about twice as many salespeople, as far as we could tell. In nearly every sales territory, there were at least two competitor reps serving the same base of customers. And it just happened that that competitor had almost exactly twice the market share of my client. From every perspective I looked at it, the math was right. The sales force needed to double its size to accomplish its goal.

When I presented this finding to the VP of sales, the conversation went like this:

VP of Sales: [laughter] There is no way this can be right. Your math must be wrong.

Me: Well, it's just math. If anything is wrong, it would have to be the assumptions that went into the calculations. But you were there when we vetted all of these assumptions with your team. Not only once, but twice.

VP: Then you must have gotten something else wrong. Your approach must be flawed.

Me: I've gone through this exercise many times with several clients, including another division of your own company. I'm pretty confident that the approach is appropriate and the numbers are correct.

[I go on to validate the headcount projections from every possible angle, including the marketplace reality checks of competitors, market share, and other anecdotal evidence.]

VP: Well, there's no way I can show these numbers to my boss. You're telling me that I need to request *double* my current headcount for next year. He'll throw me out of his office.

Me: This is what the numbers are telling us, and I don't think they're lying. If he wants to accomplish what he says he wants to accomplish in the form of market share gains, then yes, he'll need to give you twice the headcount that you have. Maybe not next year, but it should be in your mid-range plans.

VP: There's just no way. I don't believe these numbers. Our sales force is so much more efficient than our competition's. We *have* to be able to do better with no more resources than we currently have in the field.

Me: I don't see it happening. And your historical performance is on the side of the math. You're number three in the market for a reason, and it doesn't seem that it's your products' fault.

VP: Okay, here's what I need. I want you to go back and re-do these numbers. I need this coverage model to say that we should hire maybe 15% to 20% more people. That will seem credible. I can sell that to my boss.

Me: You want me to manipulate the math until it produces your desired outcome?

VP: Yes. Your assumptions must be wrong. 15-20% is more reasonable. That's what I need the model to show.

Me (trying to decide whether I will actually do this): I, umm … I'm not sure that's what you hired me to do.

VP: Well, what I hired you to do is not working out the way I need it to. I want you to make those changes. And fast.

Despite a prolonged negotiation to retain some level of mathematical integrity, the coverage model eventually yielded to the VP of sales' desires. I once had a professor who said, "If you torture the numbers long enough, they'll confess to anything." Torture them we did, and confess they did. A forced confession, of course. The kind that wouldn't hold up in a court of mathematical law.

You won't be surprised to learn that good fortune did not shine on the North American division of this company. The VP of sales was gone within a year, and the entire division was for sale within two. The division had such an undesirable market position that it took two more years before it was eventually sold to a private equity firm. In that same amount of time, it could probably have turned its fortunes around for real, if it had only respected the math.

The lesson: Math is not to be ignored. It is not to be manipulated. In the end, mathematical laws will be enforced, and the underlying reality will prevail. Always.

THE GOOD IDEAS

GOOD IDEA 1: TRUST THE MATH

There is a lot of math in the sales force. It's not complicated math—mostly just addition, subtraction, multiplication, and division. However, that math often gets influenced in one direction or another by the will of the people. Sales forecasts bend up or down and performance measures lean and stretch; and maybe that's okay for the purposes of managing expectations. But for the purposes of managing the sales force, certain decisions must be data-driven. When the decisions are important, respect the analysis and its conclusions. The math will never be wrong, but ignoring it can prove you to be.

GOOD IDEA 2: FACE REALITY

Sales forces can be very insular, and they tend to create their own realities. We think our salespeople are rock stars, when sometimes they're just average. We think our products are the best, when sometimes they kind of stink. But there are external realities that should bring us back in line, like when we always get outsold and our products get returned. You need to be optimistic, but you can't ignore reality. If you're number three in your market, then there's probably a legitimate reason. Open your eyes, identify the problems, and take corrective action. Then your reality will actually improve.

PART IV
LET'S KEEP THE PARTY GOING

CHAPTER TWENTY-THREE

THE END ... AND BEYOND!

THANKS FOR THE MEMORIES

It probably took you just a few hours to read this book, but it took me many years to live it. And during the time it took me to *write* it, I was able to enjoy a stroll down memory lane. If there's one thing I can say with confidence about my career, it's that I encountered a truly diverse and comical cast of characters.

Looking back, I got to know many of the folks in these vignettes quite well as the stories unfolded. To me, there are actual names and faces attached to the preceding chapters, and many of them are still acquaintances. Perhaps some of them will read this book and think, "Hey, I remember that story ... that *was* insane now that I think about it."

That said, most of these people surely forgot about me the very moment I turned in my temporary office keys and exited their buildings. To them I was just a passer-by, but (little did they know) I was paying very close attention. And if there was one characteristic that almost all of these people had in common, it was this: They were totally unaware of their insane behaviors. Absolutely oblivious. To them, it was just business as usual.

So thank you for the memories, everyone. *You* are the real stars of the show. I'm just the storyteller—you're the talent. Thank you for your wonderful moments of insanity. Thanks for being you.

NOW THAT YOU KNOW...

Now that you've been alerted to the existence of the sales Worst Practice and the insanity that accompanies it, you've probably come up with a few examples of your own. If not, don't worry—chances are you'll start to notice them everywhere you look. It's a phenomenon called psychological priming, like when you buy a car and suddenly every other car you see on the road looks just like yours. After reading this book, your mind is now primed to recognize insane sales behaviors.

Here's how it will go: Your day will be humming along just like any other, when you'll suddenly see someone doing something that gives you pause. The more you stare at it, the more your eyes will squint and your head will tilt sideways. Something just won't look right. Then you'll try to snap yourself out of it, assuming that you *must* be misinterpreting something. But no. You'll slowly realize that you're seeing it perfectly for what it is: Alarmingly backward behavior that is barreling toward unavoidable disaster. In fact, you'll be witnessing a bout of sales insanity.

When the moment inevitably comes, pause and soak it in. If you're distant enough from the inevitable consequences, it will be quite entertaining. Like when someone other than you falls into an open sewer and dies. It's just good clean fun.

REFERENCE GUIDE
JUST THE
GOOD IDEAS

GOOD IDEAS FOR SALES PEOPLE

SLOW DOWN

Salespeople operate at an abnormally frenetic pace. Even if it's not in their blood, it's in their environment. Daily call reports. Weekly conference calls. Monthly quotas. It's all there to make the sales force work harder. But selling is no longer about being the fastest runner—it's about running the smartest race. If you're running too fast, you will overshoot your target. Slow down. Slow. Down.

THINK

Sales is not the same as it used to be. Persuasion has been replaced with collaboration. Speed has been replaced with agility. Strength has been replaced with strategy. The salespeople who are winning today are thinkers. They are deliberate. They don't try to emulate their last successful sales call—they try to predict what will make the next one a success. Most of the salespeople I've met are smart enough to win any deal, but far fewer actually do it with any consistency. Those who do, think.

PLAN

The value of planning cannot be overstated, but it's an admittedly tedious affair. Not many people enjoy doing it, but most who do will agree that it leads to better outcomes. Whether they are planning to make a sales call or to attain some other objective, the best salespeople plan. The effort that it takes is *far* outweighed by the confidence and capability it instills in them. Knowing what to do is very powerful. So slow down, think, and plan.

NEGOTIATING SKILL IS INVALUABLE FOR A SALESPERSON

Generally speaking, there's not enough education or training for salespeople on the skill of negotiating. Unfortunately, negotiating is far down the training agenda behind product knowledge, information systems, and other more tactical things. However, this skill is so critical that salespeople should seek training themselves if necessary. The ability to negotiate goes beyond just defending your price—it is foundational to developing and demonstrating a value-added relationship with your customer.

PRICE IS ONLY ONE OF MANY SOURCES OF VALUE

Simply seeing the word 'negotiate' takes most people's minds immediately to 'price.' However, the price is typically only one component of a larger value proposition. When you find yourself in a negotiation, be sure to get all the sources of value on the table. Make certain that the customer knows what else you have to offer—what other benefits do they stand to receive? If the negotiation takes place solely on price, you have done a disservice to both yourself and to your customer.

HAVE A BACKBONE

No explanation required.

VIEW UNANTICIPATED RFP'S WITH SKEPTICISM

RFPs look like highly qualified leads, and sometimes they are. But in my experience, most times they are not. When an RFP lands in your lap, try to talk yourself out of responding to it rather than automatically assuming that you will. Really look at it with a skeptical eye. If the description of the buyer's need looks like it could have been written by a competitor, then it probably was. If the timeline seems unrealistic, then it probably is. If you don't think you are the perfect vendor to provide this work, then you probably aren't. Don't assume the best when you receive an RFP: assume the worst.

A LEAD IS NOT QUALIFIED UNLESS YOU CAN WIN IT

Classic qualification criteria for a 'good' lead are meant to ensure that the buyer is ready to spend her money. If they have a need, a budget, a timeline, and a buying process, then the stage is set for a successful purchase. But NOT necessarily for a successful sale. If the deal is unwinnable, then it's not really qualified. The buyer might be ready to buy, but that doesn't mean he's ready to buy from you. Don't let the excitement of an inevitable purchase fool you into believing that it's your inevitable sale.

RETAINING EXISTING CUSTOMERS IS MORE FUN THAN YOU THINK

In sales, we *love* to acquire new customers. A 'hunter' who brings in new business it typically praised much more loudly than a 'farmer' who retains and grows existing accounts. But make no mistake, if you're throwing parties at the front door and quietly losing customers out the back, you are doing yourself a grave disservice. It's easier to keep a customer than to win one, so don't let the good ones wash away.

DEMONSTRATE VALUE OR ELSE LOSE YOUR CUSTOMERS

Many sales forces have revenue models where prolonged customer satisfaction is somewhat irrelevant. They sell a stand-alone product to one customer and move on to the next. The fortunes of other sales forces are very closely tied to their customers' perception of value. If you rely on repeat customers for your livelihood, then you *must* demonstrate value *before* the next purchase decision. Otherwise, you'll be fighting a losing battle, because history will not be on your side.

PAY ATTENTION TO THE DETAILS

Salespeople live in a chaotic, hurried environment. There's never enough time to complete all of their tasks, and any opportunity to take a shortcut can appear like a great idea. But usually it's not. Even the smallest oversights can have expensive and long-lasting consequences. If you're one of those people who likes to use the "Replace All" function in your word processor, then sales might be a dangerous career for you. When customers are involved, the details matter. A lot.

BIGGER ISN'T NECESSARILY BETTER

There is an intuitive appeal to bigger customers. And all things being equal, they tend to be better for you, too. But not always. Sometimes your biggest customers might also be your worst, because they're either less profitable, less strategic, or just more annoying. Be sure to understand the type of customers you want, and then do what you can to attract and retain those. You don't need every customer, just the ones that are good for your company.

BEWARE THE 'MARKET PRICE'

The 'market price' is a customer euphemism for the lowest price that anyone has ever spoken aloud. Don't lead a race to the bottom just because someone tells you a lower price exists. You shouldn't have to give away your products—they deserve a price that reflects the true value you provide to your customers. If your customers won't buy at a price that you want to sell, then politely walk away. Let 'the market' have the business instead.

YOU MIGHT HAVE TO FIRE A CUSTOMER

Salespeople spend most of their energy trying to acquire and grow customers, so it's almost unthinkable to purposefully end an active customer relationship. But like any relationship, some customers who start out as a dream will end up a nightmare. If they're a bad customer to you, hopefully they'll be an even worse customer to your competitor. Let them be just that.

TECHNICAL DETAILS MATTER LESS TO THE BUYER

Despite the high level of technical expertise you possess as a seller, buyers care most about solving their own problems. And those problems are inevitably functional in nature, not technical. Fight the desire to share all the gory technical details until you've demonstrated that you can solve the customer's functional problem. Then perhaps the buyer will be interested enough to ask for a deeper dive into your solution.

IMPRESS THE BUYER, NOT YOURSELF

It feels great to be the expert, and it feels even better to show someone else how much of an expert you are. But the buyer is the one who needs to be elevated during a sales interaction, not the seller. A sales call is not the time to impress yourself or your colleagues—it's a time to impress upon the buyer that you can relieve their pain and lead them to a better place. Buyers need experts who can *apply* their expertise, not just revel in it.

INSTITUTIONALIZE INTIMACY WITH YOUR MOST VALUABLE CUSTOMERS

If a minority of your customers constitute the majority of your business, you must stay engaged with them at a very deep level. Put formal procedures in place to learn what they're thinking and what they need at all times. Familiarity leads to complacency, and complacency leads to neglect. Have frequent, meaningful conversations, or else risk losing your customers' allegiance to their new best friend: your competitor.

ASSUME YOUR COMPETITORS ARE ALWAYS LURKING

If you have customers that buy from you on an ongoing basis, it's tempting to believe that they will be loyal forever. And the longer your relationships last, the more loyalty you might expect. However, your competitors are smart enough to find your customers, and your customers are smart enough to entertain a better deal. If a better offer comes along, they just might take it. Then you'll be the one lurking around, searching for a way back in.

DON'T ASSUME YOU KNOW WHAT BUYERS ARE THINKING

Part of the sales challenge is to uncover buyers' needs, so you can then try to satisfy them. As a corollary, you also have to uncover their objections, so you can try to dispel them. But you can't pretend to know what your prospects are thinking— you have to ask them questions to uncover the truth. Making assumptions about their state of mind or their state of affairs is high-risk behavior. Behavior that will cost you sales.

NEVER RAISE OBJECTIONS ON BEHALF OF BUYERS

During the course of a sale, there will be plenty of forces campaigning against you—ferocious competitors, skeptical buyers, and market detractors, just to name a few. Don't join their team. There's nothing to be gained by printing your own bad press. Raising objections on behalf of your prospects won't make you appear more proactive or credible. It will just make you appear more objectionable.

THE SELLER MUST DO THE HEAVY LIFTING IN A SALES CALL

There may be two people involved in a typical sales call, but the burden of a productive meeting is not split between them. The burden lies fully with the seller to facilitate value creation for the buyer. Blaming the buyer for a failed sales call is the worst type of delusion, because it vindicates the person responsible for the failure and blames the person who was the unwitting victim of sales malpractice. When you leave a failed sales call, don't bemoan the buyer's ignorance. Find the nearest mirror and ask it what really went wrong.

SELLING INNOVATION REQUIRES AN ADVANCED SKILL SET

As much as we deride the show-up-and-throw-up salesperson as a relic of the past, the truth is that many salespeople still can (and do) succeed by playing the role of a feature-and-function robot. But when it's time to sell a disruptive technology or innovation, those sales reps will fail miserably. The ability to pull buyers delicately down the path from a world they know to a world they *could* know is beyond many sellers. It requires a level of restraint and awareness that is counter to the way many sellers view themselves. If you're launching a truly innovative product, think carefully about which of your salespeople are up to the task and which ones will merely leave your prospects flummoxed.

THE BUYER IS OFTEN MORE MOTIVATED THAN THE SELLER

Buyers are the ones with the actual problems, and they want those problems resolved. By the time they enter into a buying process, they're typically committed to acquiring a solution. They might not be committed to buying it from *you*, but they want to buy it from someone. Take what they say at face value, unless you have a reason to believe they're lying. They have more to lose than you do if the sale goes wrong.

IT'S BETTER TO MEET YOUR BUYER'S DEMANDS THAN TO DEMAND THEY MEETS YOURS

There is give-and-take between the buyer and seller in almost every complex sale. But remember this truth: The seller exists to solve the buyer's problem, not vice versa. If the buyer continues to pull you in their direction, then it's often best to yield your position. Pull too hard and the buyer will give up. You'll be left with nothing, and the buyer will simply find someone to replace you. Your competitor's salespeople are remarkably easy to locate.

GOOD IDEAS FOR SALES MANAGERS

TECHNOLOGY IS JUST AN ENABLER OF BUSINESS PROCESSES

Technology is too often sold as the silver bullet cure-all for any business issue. In reality, technology is just an enabler. It won't solve any problems on its own—it will just help you do the wrong things faster. Attempting to automate chaos is one classic foible, as is assuming that a new system will provide you with embedded Best Practices. Take the time to define how you want your business to work *before* you set about automating it. Otherwise, a technology implementation could become a very expensive and disruptive way to ruin your career.

WHEN IMPLEMENTING TECHNOLOGY, THINK SMALL

'Big bang' system implementations are always tinged with insanity. My counsel to clients is always the same: Implement the smallest piece of technology that you can possibly imagine, and then build the functionality in bite-sized pieces. If you're replacing your current CRM tool, start by replicating the existing tool's functionality. If you're implementing a tool for the first time, think very carefully about which critical activities you really need to automate. Then add the bells and whistles. Otherwise, the sound you hear won't be all the bells and whistles working in the background, it will be sound of an oncoming train.

THE SALES FORCE IS THE CUSTOMER EXPERIENCE

Companies should never lose sight of one important fact: At the beginning of every customer relationship, the salesperson defines the company in the buyer's eyes. No matter how good a company's products, and no matter how strong its brand, the sales force *is* the customer experience as the relationship begins. Degrade the sales force at your own peril.

GOOD SALESPEOPLE ARE WORTH EVERY PENNY

It seems to me that there are two types of people: Those who think salespeople should never make more money than their managers, and those who think salespeople should make more money than their CEO. I've always considered the latter type to be the saner group of folks. Every company should acknowledge that its fortunes are derived from the people on the front lines. Don't begrudge top salespeople for earning lots of money, congratulate them and say "thank you" for a job well done.

PRODUCTIVITY = EFFICIENCY X EFFECTIVENESS

The output of your sales force is driven by both its efficiency and its effectiveness. Efficiency is about prioritizing your activities wisely; Effectiveness is about being good at what you do. Smart sales leaders will pay equal attention to both. Without one, you're wasting time. Without the other, you're wasting effort. Neither of those is a productive way to manage your sales force.

SALES SUPPORT IS CHEAP

With the exception of senior management, salespeople are typically the most expensive resources in any company. Administrative support is often the cheapest. If there's any way to offload low-value tasks from your sales team to support staff, then do it today. The increase in efficiency will be almost immediate, and you might even boost your effectiveness too. Don't ask any questions—don't even ask for permission. Just do it. It might be the only Current Best Practice that I will abide.

COMMUNICATION ACROSS SALES TEAMS IS A GOOD THING

This is kind of obvious, but if your growth strategy is to have your sales teams cross-sell various products and services, silos are a death wish. You must do everything possible to enable each group to sell the others' wares, which includes having a clear understanding of the features, functions, value propositions, and buying processes for the complementary products. Direct communication among the sellers is a great way for them to learn—perhaps even better than formalized training.

MOTIVATION CAN TAKE YOU ONLY SO FAR

It doesn't take much to motivate a sales force—at least in the near term. Whether you use a carrot or a stick, salespeople are relatively excitable. The problem is that once you get your sellers running as fast as they possibly can, motivation fails to make an incremental impact. At some point, you need to help your salespeople become better runners. Otherwise, they'll either run into a wall or run to your competitor. And that's no good for anyone.

ORGANIZE YOUR SALES FORCE FOR YOUR CUSTOMERS

There's an old saying that the customer is always right. Well, of course the customer is *not* always right ... but the customer is still the customer. You need to accommodate your customers, not force your will upon them, and the customers' experience begins with the way you organize your sales force around them. Be attentive to the way your customers want to be served, and serve them in that way. It will be an all-around more pleasant experience.

DON'T COMPETE WITH YOURSELF

Most salespeople are competitive by nature, and their competitive drive can be a strong motivator. They compete against one another for recognition and status within the sales force, but they should never have to compete for the same customer. Some people might view such a competition as "we win either way." I view it as a "you lose either way." If there's any true winner, it might be the customer, but their victory will come with an economic and cultural cost to your company.

THE SELLING PROCESS MUST MIRROR THE BUYING PROCESS

Sales forces are fixated on sales processes and the consistent execution of sales activities ... and they should be. However, they shouldn't forget that the real task of a salesperson is to help a buyer buy. If your selling activities are misaligned with the buying activities on the other side of the handshake, then you're placing unnecessary obstacles in the way. Start with the buying process and build your selling process backward from there. Then sales will happen on a natural course.

THE BUYER IS IN CONTROL—ALWAYS

Salespeople are expected to be aggressive. Sometimes that's a good thing, because it gives sellers the confidence to drive a sale forward. But sometimes it's a bad thing, because it gives sellers the false sense that they are in control of the buyer's decision-making process. The buyer is *always* in control of the decision-making process, because she's the only one who can decide to buy. Ignore this fact at your own economic peril.

SET YOUR SALES TARGETS CAREFULLY

Sales targets can be set in a number of ways, from the top-down allocation of the company's target to field-level negotiations between sellers and their managers. However you choose to go about it, make sure your salespeople's performance targets are viewed as achievable. You want to motivate your sellers to high levels of performance, but you don't want to set them on a path to assured failure. When targets are set properly, your top performers will reach them and your bottom performers won't. But they should nevertheless be motivated to try.

CREATE A CULTURE OF SUCCESS

People like to succeed, and success is contagious. Don't be afraid to feed a culture of success by setting your sellers up to win. And when they do, celebrate their victories loudly. Once your salespeople's sails are full of wind, they'll tend to pick up speed, and the resulting revenue regatta will be a beautiful thing to watch. It sure beats watching your fleet of boats sitting dead in the water, with no wind in the forecast.

SALESPEOPLE SHOULD NOT BE TREATED AS LONE WOLVES

Many salespeople like to think of themselves as lone wolves, but in reality they tend to be more successful when they work in a pack. Organizational and marketplace dynamics are increasingly complicated, and sellers that don't communicate or collaborate will develop large blind spots. They'll bounce around and nip at each other until the lack of coordination creates a sales force that equals less than the sum of its parts. But when sellers operate as a cohesive team to share insights and resources, everyone is much more likely to prosper.

SALES MANAGERS MATTER ... A LOT

Sales managers are the leaders of the pack, and they keep their individual sellers healthy, wealthy, and wise. They have the unique ability to corral and coordinate team members and to apply organizational resources where needed. A good sales management team is worth its weight in gold, because it drives greater productivity across the entire sales force. Discount your sales managers and you will be discounting your team's performance. Celebrate your managers, and you will be toasting to your future success.

COMPENSATION PLANS MUST WORK FOR BOTH SALESPEOPLE AND MANAGEMENT

Compensation is extremely important to everyone in the sales force. For salespeople, it represents success, prosperity, and stature. For management, it serves to align, motivate, and reward. When designing a sales compensation plan, both perspectives are critical to consider. Treat it purely as remuneration for sellers, and you lose the ability to guide the sales force. Treat it purely as a control mechanism for management, and you lose the ability to inspire performance. Balance both, and you'll have a sales team that will run really hard in precisely the right direction.

DON'T OVER-ENGINEER SALES COMPENSATION

When designing compensation plans, most sales leaders struggle with simplicity. It's easy to jam more and more stuff into a compensation plan, assuming that your salespeople will heed the various signals and give you all the things you want. But the exact opposite is true. The more objectives you squeeze into a compensation plan, the more noise you broadcast to the field. Eventually, your salespeople will recognize it as such and begin to tune it out.

INCENTIVE COMPENSATION SHOULD MOTIVATE AND REWARD, NOT PUNISH

The reason that incentive plans aren't called dis-incentive plans is kind of obvious: They're meant to inspire good performance, not to censure bad behavior. If you want to discourage petty crimes in your sales force, do so through rigorous sales management and disciplinary action. If you want to drive sales results, do so through clear direction and generous rewards. Attempting to do both through a single compensation plan sends mixed signals and dampens the very enthusiasm that you're trying to create.

TRUST THE MATH

There is a lot of math in the sales force. It's not complicated math—mostly just addition, subtraction, multiplication, and division. However, that math often gets influenced in one direction or another by the will of the people. Sales forecasts bend up or down and performance measures lean and stretch; and maybe that's okay for the purposes of managing expectations. But for the purposes of managing the sales force, certain decisions must be data-driven. When the decisions are important, respect the analysis and its conclusions. The math will never be wrong, but ignoring it can prove you to be.

FACE REALITY

Sales forces can be very insular, and they tend to create their own realities. We think our salespeople are rock stars, when sometimes they're just average. We think our products are the best, when sometimes they kind of stink. But there are external realities that should bring us back in line, like when we always get outsold and our products get returned. You need to be optimistic, but you can't ignore reality. If you're number three in your market, then there's probably a legitimate reason. Open your eyes, identify the problems, and take corrective action. Then your reality will actually improve.